Tudor and Stuart Drama

GOLDENTREE BIBLIOGRAPHIES
In Language and Literature
under the series editorship of
O. B. Hardison, Jr.

Tudor and Stuart Drama

SECOND EDITION

compiled by

Irving Ribner

and

Clifford Chalmers Huffman

State University of New York at Stony Brook

AHM Publishing Corporation
Arlington Heights, Illinois 60004

ISBN: 0-88295-554-3, paper
ISBN: 0-88295-572-1, cloth

Library of Congress Card Number: 76-5215

PRINTED IN THE UNITED STATES OF AMERICA
788

Contents

CONTENTS

Preface

The second edition of the *Goldentree Bibliography of Tudor and Stuart Drama* is intended, like its predecessor, for both advanced undergraduates and graduate students who desire a convenient guide to scholarship in the field of English Renaissance Drama. The number of books and articles devoted to this field appearing annually has escalated so steadily over the past decade that the following list by necessity continues to be selective. However, the editors have made every effort to provide ample coverage of the major studies, with emphasis on work published in the period 1920–75. Many items have been added to this edition, even among older titles, and studies written in foreign languages have been included where it seemed reasonable to expect that they may be available in university libraries.

Among the exclusions are:

1. General "background" studies unless they deal significantly and specifically with the major playwrights and their plays.
2. Articles the substance of which was later incorporated into books.
3. Selections of plays for classroom use and collections of essays which had appeared earlier in learned journals.
4. Anonymous plays. (Until recently, scholarly attention to these tended to confine itself to authorship-attribution studies. See the contribution by Anne Lancashire and Jill Levenson to *The Predecessors of Shakespeare: A Survey and Bibliography of Recent Studies in English Renaissance Drama,* Terence P. Logan and Denzell S. Smith, eds. (Lincoln: University of Nebraska Press, 1972), pp. 161–311.)
5. Unpublished material: the student is directed to *Dissertation Abstracts, Microfilm Abstracts* and *Research Opportunities in Renaissance Drama.*

This edition of the *Goldentree Bibliography of Tudor and Stuart Drama* seeks to be of the widest possible use. For each of the Major Authors, the listing begins with specialized bibliographies and the major scholarly editions of the complete or selected works, and of individ-

vii

ual plays. The critical works on the playwright in question appear alphabetically according to the last name of the scholar. Some attention has been given to textual studies, which may affect critical interpretation; however, for more specialized treatments of textual bibliography, the student is referred to the journals *The Library, Studies in Bibliography* and *Papers of the Bibliographical Society of America.* An annual survey of such studies appears in *Manuscripta.*

In general, Professor Ribner attempted to steer a middle course between the brief lists of references included in the average textbook and the long professional bibliography used by advanced research scholars, in which significant items may be lost in the sheer number of entries. In preparing the revised edition, I have followed Professor Ribner's lead, although the volume of publication since the first edition has resulted in almost twice as many items. I have recorded only the first appearances of these books and articles, many of which have subsequently been reprinted. While each reader will devise his own manner of using this compilation, it may be helpful to note that the first parts include general studies and more specific ones arranged by topic, thus providing a context for treatments of individual playwrights and plays. The student doing research on a playwright should consult not only the works arranged under his name, but also those in the appropriate generic section (tragedy or comedy, for instance) and in the "General Studies." It is hoped that this bibliography will assist students in their efforts to survey a field of knowledge, to write reports and term papers, prepare for examinations and to do independent reading.

Journals which appear with any frequency are cited in abbreviated form; a key appears just after the table of contents. One final note: Cambridge as a place of publication is Cambridge, England for Cambridge University Press, and Cambridge, Massachusetts for Harvard University Press.

The compilation of this bibliography has been materially helped by the generosity of the Graduate School of S.U.N.Y. at Stony Brook; thanks are also due to Mrs. Bonnie Hoffman for many hours of cheerful and unflagging assistance.

Clifford Chalmers Huffman

Abbreviations

AI	American Imago
AntigR	Antigonish Review
ArielE	Ariel: A Review of International English Literature
BJRL	Bulletin of the John Rylands Library
BNYPL	Bulletin of the New York Public Library
BSUF	Ball State University Forum
BUSE	Boston University Studies in English
CE	College English
CL	Comparative Literature
CLAJ	College Language Association Journal
ClioW	Clio: An Interdisciplinary Journal of Literature, History, and the Philosophy of History
CompD	Comparative Drama
CR	The Critical Review
DramaS	Drama Survey
DUJ	Durham University Journal
EA	Études Anglaises
E&S	Essays and Studies by Members of the English Association
EIC	Essays in Criticism
ELH	ELH: A Journal of English Literary History
ELN	English Language Notes
ELR	English Literary Renaissance
ES	English Studies
ESA	English Studies in Africa
ETJ	Educational Theatre Journal
FurmS	Furman Studies
HAB	Humanities Association Bulletin
HLB	Harvard Library Bulletin
HLQ	Huntington Library Quarterly
HR	Hispanic Review
HussR	Husson Review
JEGP	Journal of English and Germanic Philology
JHI	Journal of the History of Ideas
JMRS	Journal of Medieval and Renaissance Studies
JWCI	Journal of the Warburg and Courtauld Institute
LCrit	Literary Criterion
MHRev	Malahat Review
MLN	Modern Language Notes
MLQ	Modern Language Quarterly

MLR	Modern Language Review
MQR	Michigan Quarterly Review
MP	Modern Philology
MSE	Massachusetts Studies in English
MSpr	Moderna Språk
MuK	Maske und Kothurn
N & Q	Notes and Queries
NLH	New Literary History
PBSA	Papers of the Bibliographical Society of America
PCP	Pacific Coast Philology
PLL	Papers on Language and Literature
PMLA	Publications of the Modern Language Association of America
PQ	Philological Quarterly
PTRSC	Proceedings and Transactions of the Royal Society of Canada
QJS	Quarterly Journal of Speech
QRL	Quarterly Review of Literature
RenD	Renaissance Drama
RenP	Renaissance Papers
RenQ	Renaissance Quarterly (Formerly *Renaissance News*)
RES	Review of English Studies
RLC	Revue de Littérature Comparée
RLV	Revue des Langues Vivantes
RMS	Renaissance and Modern Studies
RORD	Research Opportunities in Renaissance Drama
RSH	Revue des Sciences Humaines
SAB	South Atlantic Bulletin
SAQ	South Atlantic Quarterly
SB	Studies in Bibliography
SEL	Studies in English Literature, 1500–1900
SFQ	Southern Folklore Quarterly
ShJ	Shakespeare Jahrbuch
ShN	Shakespeare Newsletter
SHR	Southern Humanities Review
ShakS	Shakespeare Studies
ShStud	Shakespeare Studies (Japan)
SoQ	The Southern Quarterly
SoR	Southern Review
SoRA	Southern Review: An Australian Journal of Literary Studies
SP	Studies in Philology
SQ	Shakespeare Quarterly
SR	Sewanee Review
SRO	Shakespearean Research Opportunities
SS	Shakespeare Survey
TDR	The Drama Review (formerly *Tulane Drama Review*)
TLS	Times Literary Supplement (London)
TN	Theatre Notebook
TS	Theatre Survey
TSL	Tennessee Studies in Literature
TSLL	Texas Studies in Literature and Language

ABBREVIATIONS

UMSE	University of Mississippi Studies in English
UTQ	University of Toronto Quarterly
UTSE	University of Texas Studies in English
WVUPP	West Virginia University Philological Papers
YES	Yearbook of English Studies
YR	Yale Review

NOTE: The publisher and compiler invite suggestions for new entries in future editions of the bibliography.

Basic Works of Reference, Textual and Historical

1 ADAMS, Joseph Quincy. *The Dramatic Records of Sir Henry Herbert.* New Haven: Yale University Press, 1917.

2 ARBER, Edward, ed. *A Transcript of the Registers of the Company of Stationers of London: 1554–1640.* 5 vols. London: Privately printed, 1875–77. Reprinted, New York: P. Smith, 1950.

3 BARROLL, J. Leeds, *et al.*, eds. *Revels History of Drama in English III: 1576–1613.* New York: Barnes and Noble, 1974.

4 BENTLEY, Gerald Eades. *The Jacobean and Caroline Stage.* 7 vols. Oxford: The Clarendon Press, 1941–68.

5 CHAMBERS, E. K. *The Elizabethan Stage.* 4 vols. Oxford: The Clarendon Press, 1923.

6 COLLIER, John Payne. *A History of English Dramatic Poetry to the Time of Shakespeare.* 3 vols. London: J. Murray, 1831.

7 CUNNINGHAM, Peter. *Extracts from the Accounts of the Revels at Court, in the Reigns of Queen Elizabeth and James I, from the Original Office Books of the Masters and Yeoman.* London: Shakespeare Society Publications, 7, 1842.

8 FEUILLERAT, Albert, ed. *Documents Relating to the Office of the Revels in the Time of Queen Elizabeth.* Materialien zur Kunde des alteren Englischen Dramas, 21. Louvain: Uystpruyst, 1908.

9 FEUILLERAT, Albert, ed. *Documents Relating to the Revels at Court in the Time of King Edward VI and Queen Mary.* Materialien sur Kunde des alteren Englischen Dramas, 44. Louvain: Uystpruyst, 1914.

10 FLEAY, Frederick Gard. *A Biographical Chronicle of the English Drama, 1559–1642.* 2 vols. London: Reeves & Turner, 1891.

11 GREG, W. W. *A Bibliography of the English Printed Drama to the Restoration.* 4 vols. London: The Bibliographical Society, 1939–59.

12 GREG, W. W. *A List of English Plays Written Before 1643 and Printed Before 1700.* London: The Bibliographical Society, 1900.

13 HALLIWELL-PHILLIPS, James O. *A Dictionary of Old English Plays in Print or in Manuscript.* 2 vols. London: J. R. Smith, 1860.

14 HARBAGE, Alfred B. *Annals of English Drama, 975–1700.* Rev. by S. Schoenbaum. London: Methuen; Philadelphia: University of Pennsylvania Press, 1964.

15 HAZLITT, W. Carew. *The English drama and stage, under the Tudor and Stuart Princes, 1543–1664; illustrated by a series of documents, treatises, and poems.* London: The Roxburghe Library, 1869.

16 HAZLITT, W. Carew, ed. *Handbook to the Popular, Poetical, and Dramatic Literature of Great Britain from the Invention of Printing to the Restoration.* London: J. R. Smith, 1867.

17 HAZLITT, W. Carew. *A Manual for the Collector and Amateur of Old English Plays.* London: J. R. Smith, 1892.

17A HENSLOWE, Philip. *Henslowe's Diary.* Ed. by W. W. Greg. 2 vols. London: The Bibliographical Society, 1904–8.

18 HENSLOWE, Philip. *Henslowe's Diary.* Ed. by R. A. Foakes and R. T. Rickert. Cambridge: Cambridge University Press, 1961.

19 LANGBAINE, Gerard. *An Account of the English Dramatic Poets.* Oxford: G. West, 1691.

20 POLLARD, A. W. and G. R. REDGRAVE, eds. *A Short-Title Catalogue of Books Printed in England, Scotland, and Ireland.* London: The Bibliographical Society, 1926.

21 SCHELLING, F. E. *Elizabethan Drama, 1558–1642.* 2 vols. Boston: Houghton & Mifflin, 1908.

22 STEELE, Mary. *Plays and Masques at Court During the Reigns of Elizabeth, James, and Charles.* New Haven: Yale University Press, 1926.

23 WALLACE, Charles W. *The Evolution of the English Drama up to Shakespeare; with a History of the First Blackfriars Theatre.* Berlin: G. Reimer, 1912.

24 WARD, A. W. *A History of English Dramatic Literature to the Death of Queen Anne.* Rev. ed., 3 vols. London: Macmillan, 1899.

25 WELLS, Henry W. *A Chronological List of Extant Plays Produced in or About London 1581–1642.* New York: Columbia University Press, 1940.

26 WOODWARD, Gertrude L., and James G. MCMANAWAY. *A Checklist of English Plays, 1641–1700.* Chicago: University of Chicago Press, 1945.

27 WRIGHT, Louis B. *Middle-Class Culture in Elizabethan England.* Chapel Hill: University of North Carolina Press, 1935. Reprinted, Ithaca: Cornell University Press, 1958.

Anthologies and Reprint Series

28 *Anchor Anthology of Jacobean Drama.* Richard C. Harrier, ed. 2 vols. Garden City, N.J.: Doubleday, Anchor Books, 1963.

29 *Chief British Dramatists; Excluding Shakespeare.* Brander Matthews and Paul Robert Lieder, eds. Boston: Houghton Mifflin, 1924.

30 *Chief Pre-Shakespearian Dramas.* Joseph Quincy Adams, ed. Boston: Houghton Mifflin, 1924.

31 *A Collection of Old English Plays.* A. H. Bullen, ed. 4 vols. London: Bullen, 1882–5.

32 *Disputed Plays of William Shakespeare.* W. Kozlenko, ed. New York: Hawthorne, 1974.

33 *Drama of the English Renaissance.* Russell A. Fraser and Norman Rabkin, eds. 2 vols. New York: Macmillan, 1976.

34 *Early English Classical Tragedies.* John W. Cunliffe, ed. Oxford: The Clarendon Press, 1912.

35 *Early English Dramatics.* John S. Farmer, ed. 13 vols. London: privately printed, 1905–8.

ANTHOLOGIES AND REPRINT SERIES

36 *Early Plays from the Italian.* R. Warwick Bond, ed. Oxford: The Clarendon Press, 1911.

37 *Early Seventeenth-Century Plays.* H. P. Walley and J. H. Wilson, eds. New York: Harcourt, Brace, 1930.

38 *Elizabethan Dramatists Other than Shakespeare.* E. H. C. Oliphant, ed. New York: Prentice-Hall, 1931.

39 *Elizabethan Plays, Written by Shakespeare's Friends, Colleagues, Rivals and Successors.* Hazelton Spencer, ed. Boston: Little, Brown, 1933.

40 *Elizabethan and Stuart Plays.* Charles R. Baskervill, V. B. Heltzel, and A. H. Nethercot, eds. New York: Henry Holt & Co., 1934.

41 *The English Drama, 900–1642.* E. W. Parks and R. C. Beatty, eds. New York: Norton, 1935.

42 *English Drama 1580–1642.* C. F. Tucker Brooke and N. B. Paradise, eds. Boston: Heath, 1933.

43 *English Miracle Plays, Moralities and Interludes.* A. W. Pollard, ed. 7th ed. New York: Oxford University Press, 1923.

44 *Five Elizabethan Tragedies.* A. K. McIlwraith, ed. Oxford: Oxford University Press, 1938.

45 *Five Pre-Shakespearean Comedies.* F. S. Boas, ed. Oxford: Oxford University Press, 1934.

46 *Five Stuart Tragedies.* A. K. McIlwraith, ed. Oxford: Oxford University Press, 1953.

47 *Lost Plays of Shakespeare's Age.* C. J. Sisson, ed. 1936. Reprinted, New York: Humanities Press, 1970.

48 *Malone Society Reprints.* Oxford: Oxford University Press, 1906–.

49 *Materialien zur Kunde des älteren Englischen Dramas.* 44 vols. W. Bang, ed. Louvain: Uystpruyst 1902–14.

50 *Materials for the Study of the Old English Drama.* Henry De Vocht, ed. Louvain: Uystpruyst 1927–.

51 *Regents Renaissance Drama Series.* Cyrus Hoy and Gerald Eades Bentley, eds. Lincoln: University of Nebraska Press, 1963–71.

52 *Representative English Comedies.* Charles M. Gayley, ed. 4 vols. New York: Macmillan, 1903–36.

53 *Representative Medieval and Tudor Plays.* R. S. Loomis and Henry W. Wells, eds. New York: Sheed & Ward, 1942.

54 *The Revels Plays.* Clifford Leech, ed. London: Methuen; Cambridge: Harvard University Press, 1958–.

55 *A Select Collection of Old English Plays.* Robert Dodsley, ed. Rev. by W. Carew Hazlitt. 14 vols. 4th ed. London: Reeves, 1874–6.

56 *Shakespeare and His Fellow Dramatists.* E. H. C. Oliphant, ed. 2 vols. New York: Prentice-Hall, 1921.

57 *The Shakespeare Apocrypha.* C. F. Tucker Brooke, ed. Oxford: The Clarendon Press, 1908.

58 *Shakespeare's Predecessors: Selections from Heywood, Udall, Sackville and Norton, Lyly, Greene, Kyd and Marlowe.* F. J. Tickner, ed. London: Nelson, 1930.

3

59 *Specimens of the Pre-Shakespearian Drama.* J. M. Manly, ed. 2 vols. Boston: Ginn & Co., 1897. Reprinted, New York: Dover, 1967.

60 *Ten Elizabethan Plays.* Edwin Johnston Howard, ed. London: Nelson, 1935.

61 *Tudor Facsimile Texts of Old English Plays.* John S. Farmer, ed. London: Privately printed, 1907–14.

62 *Tudor Plays.* Edmund Creeth, ed. Garden City, N.J.: Doubleday, Anchor Books, 1966.

63 *Typical Elizabethan Plays.* F. E. Schelling, ed. New York: Harper, 1926.

Bibliographical Guides

64 *Abstracts of English Studies.* Boulder: University of Colorado, 1958–.

64A DONOVAN, Dennis, ed. *Thomas Dekker, 1945–1965; Thomas Heywood, 1938–1965; Cyril Tourneur, 1945–1965.* Elizabethan Bibliographies Supplements 2. London: Nether Press, 1967.

65 DONOVAN, Dennis, ed. *Thomas Middleton, 1939–1965; John Webster, 1940–1965.* Elizabethan Bibliographies Supplements 1. London: Nether Press, 1967.

66 GUFFEY, George R., ed. *Robert Herrick, 1949–1965; Ben Jonson, 1947–1965; Thomas Randolph, 1949–1965.* Elizabethan Bibliographies Supplements 3. London: Nether Press, 1968.

67 JOHNSON, Robert C., ed. *Christopher Marlowe, 1946–1965.* Elizabethan Bibliographies Supplements 6. London: Nether Press, 1967.

68 JOHNSON, Robert C., ed. *Minor Elizabethans. Roger Ascham, 1946–1966; George Gascoigne, 1941–1966; John Heywood, 1944–1966; Thomas Kyd, 1940–1966; Anthony Munday, 1941–1966.* Elizabethan Bibliographies Supplements 9. London: Nether Press, 1968.

69 JOHNSON, Robert C., ed. *Robert Greene, 1945–1965; Thomas Lodge, 1939–1965; John Lyly, 1939–1965; Thomas Nashe, 1941–1965; George Peele, 1939–1965.* Elizabethan Bibliographies Supplements 5. London: Nether Press, 1968.

70 PENNEL, Charles A., and W. P. WILLIAMS, eds. *George Chapman, 1937–1965; John Marston, 1939–1965.* Elizabethan Bibliographies Supplements 4. London: Nether Press, 1968.

71 PENNEL, Charles A., and W. P. WILLIAMS, eds. *Francis Beaumont, John Fletcher, Philip Massinger, 1937–1965; John Ford, 1940–1965; James Shirley, 1955–1965.* Elizabethan Bibliographies Supplements 8. London: Nether Press, 1968.

72 *PMLA.* Annual International Bibliography.

73 STRATMAN, Carl J., *Bibliography of English Printed Drama, 1565–1900.* Carbondale: Southern Illinois University Press, 1967.

The Printing and Publication
of Plays

74 ALBRIGHT, Evelyn May. *Dramatic Publication in England, 1580–1640: A Study of Conditions Affecting Content and Form of Drama.* New York: Modern Language Association, 1927.

75 ALLEN, Don Cameron. "Some Contemporary Accounts of Renaissance Printing Methods." *The Library,* 4th series, 17 (1937), 167–71.

76 ASHE, D. J. "The Non-Shakespearean Bad Quartos as Provincial Acting Versions." *RenP 1953,* (1954), 57–62.

77 BARTLETT, Henrietta C. "Extant Autograph Material by Shakespeare's Fellow Dramatists." *The Library,* n.s., 10 (1929), 308–12.

78 BOWERS, Fredson T. "Elizabethan Proofing." *Joseph Quincy Adams Memorial Studies.* See 289.

79 BOWERS, Fredson T. "Old-Spelling Editions of Dramatic Texts." *Studies in Honor of T. W. Baldwin.* Pp. 9–15. See 269.

80 BOWERS, Fredson T. *On Editing Shakespeare and the Elizabethan Dramatists.* Philadelphia: University of Pennsylvania Library, 1955. Reprinted with additions as: *On Editing Shakespeare.* Charlottesville: University Press of Virginia, 1966.

81 BOWERS, Fredson T. "Some Relations of Bibliography to Editorial Problems." *SB,* 3 (1950), 37–62.

82 BOWERS, Fredson T. *Textual and Literary Criticism.* Cambridge: Cambridge University Press, 1959.

83 CRAIG, Hardin. "Criticism of Elizabethan Dramatic Texts." *Studies in Honor of T. W. Baldwin.* Pp. 3–8. See 269.

84 DAWSON, Giles E. "An Early List of Elizabethan Plays." *The Library,* n.s., 15 (1935), 445–56.

85 EBERLE, Gerald J. "The Composition and Printing of Middleton's *A Mad World, My Masters.*" *SB,* 3 (1950), 246–52.

86 GASKELL, Philip. *A New Introduction to Bibliography.* Oxford: The Clarendon Press, 1972.

87 GREG, W. W. *Collected Papers.* J. C. Maxwell, ed. London: Oxford University Press, 1966.

88 GREG, W. W. *Dramatic Documents from the Elizabethan Playhouses,* 2 vols. Oxford: The Clarendon Press, 1931.

89 GREG, W. W. "The Evidence of Theatrical Plots for the History of the Stage." *RES,* 1 (1925), 257–74.

90 GREG, W. W. "Prompt Copies, Private Transcripts and the 'Playhouse Scrivener'." *The Library,* 4th series, 6 (1925), 148–56.

91 GREG, W. W. "The Rationale of Copy-Text." *SB,* 3 (1950), 19–36.

92 GREG, W. W. *Some Aspects and Problems of London Publishing between 1550 and 1650.* Oxford: The Clarendon Press, 1956.

93 GREG, W. W. *Two Elizabethan Stage Abridgements: The Battle of Alcazar and Orlando Furioso.* Oxford: The Malone Society, extra volume, 1922.

94 HARBAGE, Alfred B. "Elizabethan and Seventeenth-Century Play Manuscripts." *PMLA,* 50 (1935), 687–99.

95 JEWKES, Wilfred T. *Act Division in Elizabethan and Jacobean Plays 1583–1616.* Hamden, Conn.: The Shoestring Press, 1958.

96 KIRSCHBAUM, Leo. "A Census of Bad Quartos." *RES,* 14 (1938), 20–43.

97 KIRSCHBAUM, Leo. "The Copyright of Elizabethan Plays." *The Library,* 5th series, 14 (1959), 231–50.

98 KIRSCHBAUM, Leo. "An Hypothesis Concerning the Origin of the Bad Quartos." *PMLA,* 60 (1945), 697–715.

99 KUHL, E. P. "The Stationer's Company and Censorship (1599–1601)." *The Library,* n.s., 9 (1929), 388–94.

100 McKERROW, R. B. *An Introduction to Bibliography for Literary Students.* 2d impression. Oxford: The Clarendon Press, 1928.

101 McKERROW, R. B. "The Elizabethan Printer and Dramatic Manuscripts." *The Library,* 4th series, 12 (1931), 253–75.

102 PRICE, Hereward T. "Towards a Scientific Method of Textual Criticism for the Elizabethan Drama." *JEGP,* 36 (1937), 151–67.

103 SIBLEY, Gertrude M. *The Lost Plays and Masques, 1500–1642.* Ithaca, N.Y.: Cornell University Press, 1933.

104 SISSON, C. J. "Bibliographical Aspects of Some Stuart Dramatic Manuscripts." *RES,* 1 (1925), 421–30.

105 SISSON, C. J. "The Laws of Elizabethan Copyright: The Stationers' View." *The Library,* 5th series, 15 (1960), 8–20.

106 SISSON, C. J. *Lost Plays of Shakespeare's Age.* Cambridge: Cambridge University Press, 1936.

Dramatic Companies, Theatres, Conditions of Performance

107 ADAMS, John Cranford. *The Globe Playhouse: Its Design and Equipment.* 2d ed. New York: Barnes and Noble, 1961.

108 ADAMS, John Cranford. " 'That Virtuous Fabricke'." *SQ,* 2 (1951), 3–11.

109 ADAMS, Joseph Quincy. *Shakespearean Playhouses.* Boston: Houghton Mifflin, 1917; London: Constable, 1920.

110 ALBRIGHT, Victor E. *The Shakespearian Stage.* New York: Columbia University Press, 1909.

111 ARMSTRONG, William A. "Actors and Theatres." *SS,* 17 (1964), 191–204.

112 ARMSTRONG, William A. *The Elizabethan Private Theatres: Facts and Problems.* London: Society for Theatre Research, 1958.

113 ARMSTRONG, William A. "The Enigmatic Elizabethan Stage." *English*, 13 (1961), 216–20.

114 BACHRACH, A. G. H. "The Great Chain of Acting." *Neophilologus*, 33 (1949), 160–72.

115 BALWIN, T. W. "Elizabethan Players as Tradesfolk." *MLN*, 42 (1927), 509–10.

116 BENTLEY, Gerald Eades. "Lenten Performances in the Jacobean and Caroline Theatre." *Essays on Shakespeare and Elizabethan Drama*. Pp. 351–60. **See 287.**

117 BENTLEY, Gerald Eades. *The Profession of Dramatist in Shakespeare's Time, 1590–1642*. Princeton: Princeton University Press, 1971.

118 BERRY, Herbert. "The Boar's Head Again." *Elizabethan Theatre III* Pp. 33–65. **See 284.**

119 BERRY, Herbert. "The Playhouse in the Boar's Head Inn, Whitechapel." *Elizabethan Theatre I*. Pp. 45–73. **See 282.**

120 BERRY, Herbert. "The Stage and Boxes at Blackfriars." *SP*, 63 (1966), 163–86.

121 BLAND, D. S. "Interludes in Fifteenth-Century Revels at Furnivall's Inn." *RES*, 3 (1952), 263–8.

122 BRADBROOK, M. C. *Elizabethan Stage Conditions*. Cambridge: Cambridge University Press, 1932. Reprinted, Hamden, Conn.: Archon, 1962.

123 BRADBROOK, M. C. *The Rise of the Common Player: A Study of Actor and Society in Shakespeare's England*. London: Chatto and Windus, 1962.

124 BRADBROOK, M. C. "The Status Seekers: Society and the Common Play in the Reign of Elizabeth I." *HLQ*, 24 (1961), 111–24.

125 BRADNER, Leicester. "Stages and Stage Scenery in Court Drama before 1558." *RES*, 1 (1925), 447–8.

126 BRAINES, W. W. *The Site of the Globe Playhouse, Southwark*. 2d ed., revised. London: Hodder and Stoughton, 1924.

127 BROOK, Donald. *A Pageant of English Actors*. New York: Macmillan; London: Rockliff, 1950.

128 BROWN, John Russell. "On the Acting of Shakespeare's Plays." *QJS*, 39 (1953), 477–84.

129 BROWNSTEIN, Oscar. "The Popularity of Baiting in England before 1600: A Study in Social and Theatrical History." *ETJ*, 21 (1969), 237–50.

130 CAMPBELL, Lily B. *Scenes and Machines on the English Stage During the Renaissance*. Cambridge: Cambridge University Press, 1923. Reprinted, New York: Barnes and Noble, 1960.

131 CHUTE, Marchette. *Shakespeare and His Stage*. London: University of London Press, 1953.

132 COLLEY, John Scott. "Music in the Elizabethan Private Theatres." *Yes*, 4 (1974), 62–9.

133 COLLINS, Fletcher, Jr. "The Relation of Tudor Halls to Elizabethan Public Theatres." *PQ*, 10 (1931), 313–16.

134 COWLING, George H. *Music on the Shakespearean Stage*. Cambridge: Cambridge University Press, 1913.

135 CRAIK, T. W. *The Tudor Interlude*. Leicester: University of Leicester Press, 1958.

136 CUNNINGHAM, James P. *Dancing in the Inns of Court.* London: Jordan and Sons, 1965.

137 DE BANKE, Cecile. *Shakespearean Stage Production: Then and Now.* New York: McGraw-Hill, 1953.

138 DODD, Kenneth M. "Another Elizabethan Theater in the Round." *SQ,* 21 (1970), 125–56.

139 DOLLERUP, Cay. "Danish Costume on the Elizabethan Stage." *RES,* 25 (1974): 53–8.

140 DONDO, Mathurin. "Marionettes in the Time of Shakespeare." *University of California Chronicles,* 25 (July, 1923), 356–66.

141 DOWNER, Alan S. "Prolegomena to the Study of Elizabethan Acting." *MuK,* 10 (1964), 625–36.

142 EDINBOROUGH, Arnold. "The Early Tudor Revels Office." *SQ,* 2 (1951), 19–25.

143 EDMOND, Mary. "Pembroke's Men," *RES,* 25 (1974), 129–36.

144 FOAKES, R. A. "Henslowe and the Theatre of the 1590's." *RenD,* 6 (1963), 4–6.

145 FOAKES, R. A. "The Player's Passion: Some Notes on Elizabethan Psychology and Acting." *E&S (1954), 62–77.*

146 FOAKES, R. A. "The Profession of Playwright." *Early Shakespeare.* Pp. 11–34. **See 275.**

147 FOAKES, R. A. "Tragedy of the Children's Theatres after 1600: A Challenge to the Adult Stage." *Elizabethan Theatre II.* Pp. 37–59 **See 283.**

148 GILDERSLEEVE, V. C. *Government Regulation of the Elizabethan Drama.* New York: Columbia University Press, 1908.

149 GOLDSTEIN, Leonard. "On the Transition from Formal to Naturalistic Acting in the Elizabethan and Post-Elizabethan Theater." *BNYPL,* 62 (1958), 330–49.

150 GRAVES, Thornton S. "Notes on Puritanism and the Stage." *SP,* 18 (1921), 141–69.

151 GRAVES, Thornton S. "Women on the Pre-Restoration Stage." *SP,* 22 (1925), 184–97.

152 GREEN, A. Wigfall. *The Inns of Court and Early English Drama.* New Haven: Yale University Press, 1931.

153 GREENWOOD, David. "The Staging of Neo-Latin Plays in Sixteenth-Century England." *ETJ,* 16 (1964), 311–23.

154 GURR, A. J. *The Shakespearean Stage 1574–1642.* Cambridge: Cambridge University Press, 1970.

155 HABICHT, Werner. "Tree Properties and Tree Scenes in Elizabethan Theater." *RenD,* 4 (1971), 69–92.

156 HARBAGE, Alfred B. "Elizabethan Acting." *PMLA,* 54 (1939), 685–708.

157 HARBAGE, Alfred B. *Shakespeare's Audience.* New York: Columbia University Press, 1941.

158 HARRISON, G. B. *Elizabethan Plays and Players.* London: Routledge, 1940.

159 HARRISON, Thomas P., Jr. "The Literary Background of Renaissance Poisons." *UTSE,* 27 (1948):35–67.

160 HARVEY-JELLIE, W. *Le Théâtre classique en Angleterre.* Montreal: Librairie Beauchemin, 1933.

161 HICKMAN, Ruby Mildred. *Ghostly Etiquette on the Classical Stage.* Cedar Rapids, Iowa.: Torch Press, 1938.

162 HILLE, Gertrude. "Londoner Theaterbauten zur Zeit Shakespeares. Mit einer Rekonstruktion des Fortuna-Theaters." *ShJ,* 66 (1931), 25–78.

163 HILLEBRAND, H. N. *The Child Actors.* Urbana: University of Illinois Press, 1926.

164 HODGES, C. Walter. *The Globe Restored.* 2d rev. ed. London: Oxford University Press.

165 HODGES, C. Walter. *Shakespeare's Second Globe: The Missing Monument.* New York: Oxford University Press, 1973.

166 HODGES, C. Walter. "Unworthy Scaffolds: A Theory for the Reconstruction of Elizabethan Playhouses." *SS,* 3 (1950), 83–94.

167 HOLZKNECHT, Karl J. "Theatrical Billposting in the Age of Elizabeth." *PQ,* 2 (1923), 267–81.

168 HOPPE, Harry R. "English Actors at Ghent in the Seventeenth Century." *RES,* 25 (1949), 305–21.

169 HOSLEY, Richard. "An Approach to the Elizabethan Stage." *RenD,* 6 (1963), 71–8.

170 HOSLEY, Richard. "The Discovery-Space in Shakespeare's Globe." *SS,* 12 (1959), 35–46.

171 HOSLEY, Richard. "An Elizabethan Tiring-House Facade." *SQ,* 9 (1958), 588.

172 HOSLEY, Richard. "The Origins of the Shakespearian Playhouse." *SQ,* 15 (1964), 29–40.

173 HOSLEY, Richard. "The Origins of the So-Called Elizabethan Multiple Stage." *TDR,* 12 (1968), 28–50.

174 HOSLEY, Richard. "A Reconstruction of the Second Blackfriars." *Elizabethan Theatre I.* Pp. 74–88. **See 282.**

175 HOSLEY, Richard. "Was There a Music-Room in Shakespeare's Globe?" *SS,* 13 (1960), 113–23.

176 HOTSON, Leslie. *Shakespeare's Wooden O.* London: Rupert Hart-Davis, 1959.

177 INGRAM, William. " 'Neere The Playe Howse': The Swan Theater and Community Blight." *RenD,* n.s. 4 (1972), 53–68.

178 INGRAM, William. "The Playhouse at Newington Butts." *SQ,* 21 (1970), 385–98.

179 JACQUOT, Jean, ed. *Le Lieu théâtral à la Renaissance.* Paris: Centre nationale de la Recherche Scientifique, 1964.

180 JENSEN, Ejner. "The Style of Boy Actors." *CompD,* 2 (1968), 100–14.

181 JOSEPH, Bertram. *Elizabethan Acting.* Oxford: Oxford University Press, 1951.

182 JOSEPH, Bertram. "The Elizabethan Stage and the Art of Elizabethan Drama." *ShJ,* 91 (1955), 145–60.

183 JOSEPH, Bertram. *The Tragic Actor.* London: Routledge & Kegan Paul, 1959.

184 KERNODLE, George R. *From Art to Theatre: Form and Convention in the Renaissance.* Chicago: University of Chicago Press, 1944.

185 KING, T. J. *Shakespearean Staging 1599–1642.* Cambridge: Harvard University Press, 1971.

186 KING, T. J. "The Stage in the Time of Shakespeare: A Survey of Major Scholarship." *RenD,* 4 (1971), 199–235.

187 KLEIN, David. "Elizabethan Acting." *PMLA,* 71 (1956), 280–2.

188 KOLIN, Philip C., and R. O. WYATT. "A Bibliography of Scholarship on the Elizabethan Stage since Chambers." *RORD,* 15–16 (1972–73), 33–59.

189 LATTER, D. A. "Sight-Lines in a Conjectural Reconstruction of an Elizabethan Playhouse." *ShakS,* 28 (1975), 125–35.

190 LAVIN, J. A. "Shakespeare and the Second Blackfriars." *Elizabethan Theatre III.* Pp. 66–81. **See 284.**

191 LAWRENCE, W. J. *The Elizabethan Playhouse and Other Studies.* Stratford-upon-Avon: Shakespeare Head Press, 1912. Reprinted, New York: Russell & Russell, 1963.

192 LAWRENCE, W. J. *The Physical Conditions of the Elizabethan Playhouse.* Cambridge: Harvard University Press, 1927.

193 LAWRENCE, W. J. "Bells on the Elizabethan Stage." *Fortnightly Review,* 122 (July, 1924), 59–70.

194 LAWRENCE, W. J. *Pre-Restoration Stage Studies.* Cambridge: Harvard University Press, 1927.

195 LAWRENCE, W. J. *Those Nut-Cracking Elizabethans: Studies of the Early Theatre and Drama.* London: Argonaut Press, 1935.

196 LENNAM, Trevor. "The Children of Paul's, 1551–1582." *Elizabethan Theatre* II. Pp. 20–36. **See 283.**

197 LINTHICUM, Marie C. *Costume in the Drama of Shakespeare and His Contemporaries.* Oxford: The Clarendon Press, 1936.

198 McDOWELL, John H. "Conventions of Medieval Art in Shakespearian Staging." *JEGP,* 47 (1948), 215–29.

199 MARKER, Lise-Love. "Nature and Decorum in the Theory of Elizabethan Acting." *Elizabethan Theatre II.* Pp. 87–107. **See 283.**

200 MARKER, Lise-Love. "Tudor Court Staging: A Study in Perspective." *JEGP,* 44 (1945), 194–207.

201 MEHL, Dieter. *The Elizabethan Dumb Show: The History of a Dramatic Convention.* Cambridge: Harvard University Press, 1966.

202 MILES, Bernard, and Josephine WILSON. "Three Festivals at the Mermaid Theatre." *SQ,* 5 (1954), 307–10.

203 MILLS, L. J. "The Acting in University Comedy of Early Seventeenth-Century England." *Studies in the English Renaissance Drama.* Pp. 212–30. **See 270.**

204 MITCHELL, Lee. "The Advent of Scenic Design in England." *QJS,* 23 (1937), 189–97.

205 MOORE, John Robert. "The Songs of the Public Theater in the Time of Shakespeare." *JEGP,* 28 (1929), 166–202.

206 MORSBERGER, Robert E. *Swordplay and the Elizabethan and Jacobean Stage.* Jacobean Drama Studies 37. Salzburg: Institut für Englische Sprache und Literatur, Universität Salzburg, 1974.

207 MURRAY, John Tucker. *English Dramatic Companies, 1558-1642.* 2 vols. Boston: Houghton Mifflin, 1910.

208 NAGLER, A. M. *Shakespeare's Stage.* Trans. Ralph Manheim. New Haven: Yale University Press, 1958.

209 NICOLL, Allardyce. *Masques, Mimes and Miracles.* London: Harrap, 1931.

210 NICOLL, Allardyce. "Passing Over the Stage." *SS,* 12 (1959), 47–55.

211 NICOLL, Allardyce. "Studies in the Elizabethan Stage Since 1900." *SS,* 1 (1948), 1–16.

212 NUNGEZER, Edwin. *A Dictionary of Actors and Other Persons Associated with the Public Representation of Plays in England before 1642.* New Haven: Yale University Press, 1929.

213 ORDISH, T. Fairman. *Early London Theatres* (1894). Reprinted, with a new foreword by C. Walter Hodges. New York: White Lion Publishers, 1971.

214 PATERSON, Morton. "The Stagecraft of the Revels Office During the Reign of Elizabeth as Suggested by Documents Relating to the Office." *Studies in the Elizabethan Theatre.* C. T. Prouty, ed. Hamden, Conn.: The Shoestring Press, 1963. Pp. 1–52.

215 PENNIMAN, Josiah H. *The War of the Theatres.* Philadelphia: University of Pennsylvania Press, 1897.

216 PINCISS, G. M. "The Queen's Men, 1583–1592." *TS,* 11 (1970), 59–65.

217 PINCISS, G. M. "Thomas Creede and the Repertory of the Queen's Men, 1583–1592." *MP,* 687 (1970), 321–30.

218 PROUDFOOT, Richard. "Shakespeare and the New Dramatists of the King's Men, 1606–1613." *Later Shakespeare.* Pp. 235–61. See **278.**

219 REYNOLDS, George F. "Another Principle of Elizabethan Staging." *The Manly Anniversary Studies in Language and Literature.* Chicago: Chicago University Press, 1923. Pp. 70–1.

220 REYNOLDS, George F. "The Return of the Open Stage." *Essays on Shakespeare and Elizabethan Drama.* Pp. 361–8. See **287.**

221 REYNOLDS, George F. "Staging Elizabethan Plays." *SAB,* 24 (1949), 258–63.

222 REYNOLDS, George F. *The Staging of Elizabethan Plays at the Red Bull Theater, 1605–25.* New York: Modern Language Association, 1940.

223 RHODES, R. Crompton. *The Staging of Shakespeare.* Birmingham: Cornish Bros., 1921.

224 RIEWALD, J. G. "Some Later Elizabethan and Early Stuart Actors and Musicians." *ES,* 40 (1959), 33–41.

225 RINGLER, William. "The First Phase of the Elizabethan Attack on the Stage, 1558–1579." *HLQ,* 5 (1942), 391–418.

226 ROBERTSON, Roderick. "Oxford Theatre in Tudor Times." *ETJ,* 21 (1969), 41–50.

227 ROSENBERG, Marvin. "Elizabethan Actors: Men or Marionettes?" *PMLA,* 69 (1954), 915–27.

228 ROTHWELL, W. F. "Was There a Typical Elizabethan Stage?" *SS*, 12 (1959), 15–21.

229 ROWAN, D. F. "The Cockpit-in-Court." *Elizabethan Theatre I.* Pp. 89–102. **See 282.**

230 ROWAN, D. F. "The English Playhouse: 1595–1630" *RenD*, 4 (1971), 37–51.

231 ROWAN, D. F. "A Neglected Jones/Webb Theatre Project, Part II: A Theatrical Missing Link." *Elizabethan Theatre III.* Pp. 60–73. **See 284.**

232 ROWAN, D. F. "The Staging of *The Spanish Tragedy.*" *Elizabethan Theatre V.* Pp. 112–23. **See 286.**

233 RULFS, Donald J. "Reception of Elizabethan Playwrights on the London Stage." *SP*, 46 (1949), 54–69.

234 SABOL, Andrew J. "Recent Studies in Music and English Renaissance Drama." *SRO*, 4 (1968–69). 1–15.

235 SARLOS, Robert K. "Development and Operation of the First Blackfriars Theatre." *Studies in the Elizabethan Theatre.* C. T. Prouty, ed. Hamden, Conn.: The Shoestring Press, 1963. Pp. 137–78.

236 SAUNDERS, J. W. "Staging at the Globe, 1599–1613." *SQ*, 11 (1960), 401–25.

237 SELTZER, Daniel. "The Actors and Staging." *A New Companion to Shakespeare Studies.* Kenneth Muir and S. Schoenbaum, eds. Cambridge: Cambridge University Press, 1971. Pp. 35–54.

238 SHAPIRO, Michael. "Three Notes on the Theatre at Paul's, c. 1569–1607." *TN*, 24 (1969–70), 147–54.

239 SISSON, C. J. *The Boar's Head Theatre: An Inn-Yard Theatre of the Elizabethan Age.* Revised, Stanley Wells, ed. London and Boston: Routledge & Kegan Paul, 1972.

240 SISSON, C. J. *Lost Plays of Shakespeare's Age.* Cambridge: Cambridge University Press, 1936.

241 SMITH, G. C. Moore. "The Academic Drama at Cambridge: Extracts from College Records." *Malone Society Collections, II,* 2 (1924), 150–230.

242 SMITH, G. C. Moore. *College Plays Performed at the University of Cambridge.* Cambridge: Cambridge University Press, 1923.

243 SMITH, Irwin. *Shakespeare's Blackfriars Playhouse.* New York: New York University Press, 1964.

244 SMITH, Irwin. *Shakespeare's Globe Playhouse.* New York: Scribner's, 1956.

245 SMITH, Warren D. "The Elizabethan Stage and Shakespeare's Entrance Announcements." *SQ*, 4 (1953), 405–10.

246 SOUTHERN, Richard. "The Contribution of the Interludes to Elizabethan Staging. *Essays on Shakespeare and Elizabethan Drama.* Pp. 3–14. **See 287.**

247 SOUTHERN, Richard. *The Medieval Theatre in the Round.* London: Faber and Faber, 1957.

248 SOUTHERN, Richard. "On Reconstructing a Practicable Elizabethan Public Playhouse." *SS*, 12 (1959), 22–34.

249 SOUTHERN, Richard. *The Open Stage.* New York: Theatre Arts Books, 1959.

250 STAMM, Rudolf. "Elizabethan Stage-Practice and The Transmutation of Source Material by the Dramatists." *SS*, 12 (1959), 64–70.

251 STINSON, James. "Reconstructions of Elizabethan Public Playhouses." *Studies in the Elizabethan Theatre.* C. T. Prouty, ed. Hamden, Conn.: The Shoestring Press, 1963. Pp. 53–136.

252 THALER, Alwin. "Minor Actors and Employees in the Elizabethan Theatre." *MP,* 20 (1922), 49–60.

253 THOMPSON, Elbert N. S. *The Controversy Between the Puritans and the Stage.* Yale Studies in English, 20. New Haven: Yale University Press, 1903.

254 THORNDIKE, Ashley H. *Shakespeare's Theatre.* New York: Macmillan, 1916.

255 VENEZKY, Alice S. *Pageantry on the Shakespearean Stage.* New York: Twayne, 1951.

256 WEINER, Albert B. "Elizabethan Interior and Aloft Scenes: A Speculative Essay." *TS,* 2 (1961), 15–34.

257 WICKHAM, Glynne. *Early English Stages 1300–1660.* 2 vols. in 3. New York: Columbia University Press, 1959–72.

258 WICKHAM, Glynne. *Shakespeare's Dramatic Heritage.* London: Routledge & Kegan Paul, 1969.

259 WIERUM, Ann. " 'Actors' and 'Play-Acting' in the Morality Tradition." *RenD,* n.s. 3 (1970), 189–214.

260 WILSON, F. P. "The Elizabethan Theatre." *Neophilologus,* 39 (1955), 40–58.

261 WREN, Robert M. "The Five-Entry Stage at Blackfriars." *Theatre Research/Recherches Théâtrales,* 8 (1967), 130–8.

262 WRIGHT, Louis B. "Animal Actors on the English Stage Before 1642." *PMLA,* 42 (1927), 656–69.

263 WRIGHT, Louis B. "Elizabethan Sea Drama and Its Staging." *Anglia,* 51 (1927), 104–18.

264 WRIGHT, Louis B. "Madmen as Vaudeville Performers on the Elizabethan Stage." *JEGP,* 30 (1931), 48–54.

265 WRIGHT, Louis B. "Stage Duelling in the Elizabethan Theatre." *MLR,* 22 (1927), 265–75.

266 WRIGHT, Louis B. "Variety Entertainment by Elizabethan Strolling Players." *JEGP,* 26 (1927), 294–303.

267 WRIGHT, Louis B. "Vaudeville Dancing and Acrobatics on the Elizabethan Stage." *ES,* 63 (1928), 59–76.

268 ZITNER, S. P. "Gosson, Ovid, and the Elizabethan Audience." *SQ,* 9 (1958), 206–8.

Critical and Historical Studies

Collections of Essays

269 ALLEN, Don Cameron, ed. *Studies in Honor of T. W. Baldwin.* Urbana: University of Illinois Press, 1958.

270 BENNETT, J. W., Oscar CARGILL, and Vernon HALL, Jr, eds. *Studies in the English Renaissance Drama In Memory of Karl Julius Holzknecht.* New York: New York University Press, 1959.

271 BENTLEY, Gerald Eades, ed. *The Seventeenth Century Stage: A Collection of Critical Essays.* Chicago: Chicago University Press, 1968.

272 BLISTEIN, Elmer M., ed. *The Drama of the Renaissance: Essays for Leicester Bradner.* Providence, R.I.: Brown University Press, 1970.

273 BLUESTONE, Max, and Norman RABKIN, eds. *Shakespeare's Contemporaries: Modern Studies in English Renaissance Drama.* Englewood Cliffs, N.J.: Prentice-Hall, 1961.

274 BROCKETT, O. G., ed. *Studies in Theatre and Drama: Essays in Honor of Hubert C. Heffner.* The Hague: Mouton, 1972.

275 BROWN, John Russell, and Bernard HARRIS, eds. *Early Shakespeare.* Stratford-Upon-Avon Studies 3. London: Arnold, 1961.

276 BROWN, John Russell, and Bernard HARRIS. *Jacobean Theatre.* Stratford-Upon-Avon Studies 1. London: Arnold, 1960.

277 BROWN, John Russell, and Bernard HARRIS. *Elizabethan Theatre.* Stratford-Upon-Avon Studies 9. London: Arnold, 1966.

278 BROWN, John Russell, and Bernard HARRIS. *Later Shakespeare.* Stratford-Upon-Avon Studies 8. London: Arnold, 1966.

279 CRAIG, Hardin, ed. *Essays in Dramatic Literature: In Honor of T. M. Parrott.* Princeton: Princeton University Press, 1935.

280 DAVIS, Herbert, and Helen GARDNER, eds. *Elizabethan and Jacobean Studies Presented to Frank Percy Wilson in Honour of His Seventieth Birthday.* Oxford: The Clarendon Press, 1959.

281 FORD, Boris, ed. *The Age of Shakespeare.* The Pelican Guide to English Literature 2. Baltimore: Penguin Books, 1955; revised 1963.

282 GALLOWAY, David, ed. *The Elizabethan Theatre I.* Hamden, Conn.: Archon, 1970.

283 GALLOWAY, David, ed. *The Elizabethan Theatre II.* Hamden, Conn.: Archon, 1970.

284 GALLOWAY, David, ed. *The Elizabethan Theatre III.* Hamden, Conn.: Archon, 1973.

285 HIBBARD, G. R., ed. *The Elizabethan Theatre IV.* Hamden, Conn.: Shoe String Press, 1974.

286 HIBBARD, G. R., ed. *The Elizabethan Theatre V.* Hamden, Conn.: Archon, 1975.

287 HOSLEY, Richard, ed. *Essays on Shakespeare and Elizabethan Drama in Honor of Hardin Craig.* Columbia, Mo.: University of Missouri Press, 1962.

288 KAUFMANN, R. J., ed. *Elizabethan Drama: Modern Essays in Criticism.* New York: Oxford University Press, 1961.

289 McMANAWAY, J. G., Giles E. DAWSON, and E. E. WILLOUGHBY, eds. *Joseph Quincy Adams Memorial Studies.* Washington: The Folger Library, 1948.

290 TRACI, P. J., and Marilyn L. WILLIAMSON, eds. *Essays in the Renaissance in Honor of Allan H. Gilbert. SAQ,* 71 (1972), 459–594.

291 WARD, J. A., ed. *Renaissance Studies in Honor of Carroll Camden.* Rice University Studies 60, ii. Houston, Tex.: Rice University, 1974.

292 WIMSATT, W. K., Jr., ed. *English Stage Comedy.* English Institute Essays, 1954. New York: Columbia University Press, 1955.

General Studies

293 ADAMS, Robert P. "Transformations in the Late Elizabethan Tragic Sense of Life: New Critical Approaches." *MLQ,* 35 (1974), 352–63.

294 ADKINS, Mary G. M. "A Theory About *The Life and Death of Jack Straw.*" *UTSE,* 28 (1949), 57–83.

295 ANDERSON, D. K. "The Banquet of Love in English Drama (1595–1642)." *JEGP,* 63 (1964), 422–32.

296 ANDERSON, Ruth L. "Kingship in Renaissance Drama." *SP,* 41 (1944), 136–55.

297 ARCHER, William. *The Old Drama and the New.* Boston: Small, Maynard, 1923.

298 ARMSTRONG, William A. "The Influence of Seneca and Machiavelli on the Elizabethan Tyrant." *RES,* 24 (1948), 19–35.

299 ARONSTEIN, Philip. *Das englische Renaissancedrama.* Leipzig: Teubner, 1929.

300 BABB, Lawrence. "Love Melancholy in the Elizabethan and Early Stuart Drama." *Bulletin of the History of Medicine,* 13 (1943), 117–32.

301 BABB, Lawrence. "Melancholic Villainy in the Elizabethan Drama." *Papers of the Michigan Academy of Science, Arts and Letters,* 29 (1943), 527–35.

302 BABB, Lawrence. "The Physiological Conception of Love in the Elizabethan and Early Stuart Drama." *PMLA,* 56 (1941), 1020–35.

303 BABB, Lawrence. "Scientific Theories of Grief in Some Elizabethan Plays." *SP,* 40 (1943), 502–19.

304 BABB, Lawrence. "Sorrow and Love on the Elizabethan Stage." *SAB,* 18 (1943), 127–42.

305 BAKER, Herschel. *The Wars of Truth.* Cambridge: Harvard University Press, 1952.

306 BARBER, C. L. *The Idea of Honour in the English Drama,* 1591–1700. Stockholm: Almqvist & Wiksell, 1957.

307 BARTLEY, J. O. "The Development of a Stock Character. I. The Stage Irishman to 1800." *MLR,* 37 (1942), 438–47.

308 BARTLEY, J. O. "The Development of a Stock Character: The Stage Scotsman; The Stage Welshman (to 1800)." *MLR,* 38 (1943), 279–88.

309 BASKERVILL, Charles R. *The Elizabethan Jig and Related Song Drama.* Chicago: University of Chicago Press, 1929.

310 BASKERVILL, Charles R. "Mummers' Wooing Plays in England." *MP,* 21 (1924), 225–72.

311 BASKERVILL, Charles R. "Some Evidence for Early Romantic Plays in England." *MP,* 14 (1916), 229–51, 467–512.

312 BASTIAENEN, J. A. *The Moral Tone of Jacobean and Caroline Drama.* Amsterdam: H. J. Paris, 1930.

313 BAWCUTT, N. W. " 'Policy', Machiavellianism, and the Earlier Tudor Drama." *ELR,* 1 (1971), 195–209.

314 BEITH-HALAHMI, Esther YAEL. *Angell Fayre or Strumpet Lewd: Jane Shore as an Example of Erring Beauty in 16th Century Literature.* Elizabethan & Renaissance Studies 26, 27. 2 vols. Salzburg: Institut für Englische Sprache und Literatur, Universität Salzburg, 1974.

315 BELSEY, Catherine. "Senecan Vacillation and Elizabethan Deliberation: Influence or Confluence?" *RenD,* 6 (1973), 65–88.

316 BENTLEY, Gerald Eades. "John Cotgrove's *English Treasury of Wit and Language* and the Elizabethan Drama." *SP,* 40 (1943), 186–203.

317 BERGERON, David M. "Anthony Munday, Pageant Poet to the City of London." *HLQ,* 30 (1967), 345–68.

318 BERLIN, Normand. *Thomas Sackville.* New York: Twayne, 1974.

319 BERRY, Herbert. "Italian Definitions of Tragedy and Comedy Arrive in England." *SEL,* 14 (1974), 179–88.

320 BEVINGTON, David M. *Tudor Drama and Politics.* Cambridge: Harvard University Press, 1968.

321 BINNS, J. W. "Women or Transvestites on the Elizabethan Stage? An Oxford Controversy." *Sixteenth-Century Journal* (St. Louis) 5, ii (1974), 95–120.

322 BLACKBURN, Ruth H. *Biblical Drama Under the Tudors.* The Hague: Mouton, 1971.

323 BLAYNEY, Glenn H. "Enforcement of Marriage in English Drama (1600–1650)." *PQ,* 38 (1960), 459–72.

324 BLISSETT, William. "Lucan's Caesar and the Elizabethan Villain." *SP,* 53 (1956), 553–75.

325 BOAS, F. S. *An Introduction to Stuart Drama.* Oxford: The Clarendon Press, 1946.

326 BOAS, F. S. *An Introduction to Tudor Drama.* Oxford: The Clarendon Press, 1933.

327 BOAS, F. S. *Queen Elizabeth in Drama and Related Studies.* London: Allen and Unwin, 1950.

328 BOAS, F. S. "The Soldier in Elizabethan and Later English Drama." *Essays by Divers Hands.* R. W. Chapman, ed. London: Milford, 1942. Pp. 121–56.

329 BOAS, F. S. *University Drama in The Tudor Age.* Oxford: The Clarendon Press, 1914.

330 BONI, John. "Analogous Form: Black Comedy and Some Jacobean Plays." *Western Humanities Review,* 28 (1974), 201–15.

331 BOWDEN, William R. "The Bed Trick, 1603–1642: Its Mechanics, Ethics, and Effects." *ShakS,* 5 (1969), 112–23.

332 BOWDEN, William R. *The English Dramatic Lyric, 1603–42: A Study in Stuart Dramatic Technique.* New Haven: Yale University Press, 1951.

333 BOWERS, R. H. "Some Folger Academic Drama Manuscripts." *SB,* 12 (1959), 117–30.

334 BRADBROOK, M. C. *English Dramatic Form: A History of Its Development.* New York: Barnes and Noble, 1965.

335 BRANDL, Alois. *Quellen des weltlichen Dramas in England vor Shakespeare.* Strassburg: Trübner 1898.

336 BRERETON, John LeGay. *Writings on Elizabethan Drama.* Melbourne: Melbourne University Press, 1948.

337 BRIDGES-ADAMS, W. *The Irresistible Theatre.* Cleveland: World Publishing Co., 1957.

338 BRIGGS, K. M. *The Anatomy of Puck: An Examination of Fairy Beliefs Among Shakespeare's Contemporaries and Successors.* London: Routledge & Kegan Paul, 1959.

339 BRIGGS, K. M. *Pale Hecate's Team: An Examination of the Beliefs on Witchcraft and Magic Among Shakespeare's Contemporaries and His Immediate Successors.* London: Routledge & Kegan Paul, 1962.

340 BROOKE, C. F. Tucker. *Essays on Shakespeare and Other Elizabethans.* Leicester Bradner, ed. New Haven: Yale University Press, 1948.

341 BROOKE, C. F. Tucker. "Latin Drama in Renaissance England." *ELH,* 14 (1946), 233–40.

342 BROOKE, C. F. Tucker. *The Tudor Drama.* Boston: Houghton Mifflin, 1911.

343 BROUDE, Ronald. "*Vindicta Filia Temporis:* Three English Forerunners of the Elizabethan Revenge Play." *JEGP,* 72 (1973), 489–502.

344 BROWN, Arthur. "The Play Within a Play: An Elizabethan Dramatic Device." *E&S,* (1960), 36–48.

345 BULAND, Mabel. *The Presentation of Time in the Elizabethan Drama.* New York: Henry Holt, 1912.

346 BUSBY, Olive Mary. *Studies of the Development of the Fool in the Elizabethan Drama.* New York: Oxford University Press, 1923.

347 CAMPBELL, Lily B. *Divine Poetry and Drama in Sixteenth Century England.* Cambridge University Press, 1959.

348 CANNON, Charles D. "*A Warning for Fair Women* & The Puritan Controversy." *UMSE,* 9 (1968), 85–99.

349 CARDOZO, J. L. *The Contemporary Jew in Elizabethan Drama.* Amsterdam: H. J. Paris, 1925.

350 CARPENTER, Frederick Ives. *Metaphor and Simile in the Minor Elizabethan Drama.* Chicago: Chicago University Press, 1895.

351 CARPENTER, Frederick Ives, and Nan COOKE. "Music in the *Secunda Pastorum.*" *Speculum,* 26 (1951), 696–700.

352 CAWLEY, Robert R. *The Voyagers and Elizabethan Drama.* New York: Modern Language Association, 1938.

353 CHAMBERS, E. K. *The English Folk-Play.* Oxford: The Clarendon Press, 1933.

354 CHANG, Joseph S. M. J. " 'Of Mighty Opposites': Stoicism and Machiavellianism." *RenD,* 9 (1966), 37–58.

355 CHARNEY, Maurice. " 'This Mist, My Friend, Is Mystical': Place and Time in Elizabethan Plays," in *The Rarer Action: Essays in Honor of Francis Fergusson.* A. Cheuse and R. Koffler, eds. New Brunswick, N.J.: Rutgers University Press, 1970. Pp. 24–35.

356 CHARNEY, Maurice. "The Persuasiveness of Violence in Elizabethan Plays." *RenD,* NS 2 (1969), 59–70.

357 CLARK, Andrew. *Domestic Drama: A Survey of the Origins, Antecedents and Nature of the Domestic Play in England, 1500–1640.* Jacobean Drama Studies 23. 2 vols. Salzburg: Institut für Englische Sprache und Literatur, Universität Salzburg, 1975.

358 CLARK, William Smith. *The Early Irish Stage.* Oxford: The Clarendon Press, 1955.

359 CLARKSON, P. S. and C. T. WARREN. *The Law of Property in Shakespeare and the Elizabethan Drama.* Baltimore: Johns Hopkins University Press, 1942.

360 CLOUGH, Wilson O. "The Broken English of Foreign Characters on the Elizabethan Stage." *PQ,* 12 (1933), 255–68.

361 COLEMAN, Edward D. *The Bible in English Drama.* New York: New York Public Library, 1931.

362 COLEMAN, Edward D. "The Jew in English Drama: An Annotated Bibliography." *BNYPL,* 42 (1938), 827–50, 919–32; 42 (1939), 45–52, 374–8; 64 (1940), 361–72, 429–44, 495–504, 543–58, 620–34, 675–98, 777–88, 843–66.

363 COPE, Jackson I. "The Rediscovery of Anti-Form in Renaissance Drama." *CompD,* 1 (1967), 155–71.

364 COPE, Jackson I. *The Theatre and the Dream: From Metaphor to Form in Renaissance Drama.* Baltimore: Johns Hopkins University Press, 1973.

365 CRAIG, Hardon. *The Enchanted Glass: The Elizabethan Mind in Literature.* New York: Oxford University Press, 1936; Reprinted, 1950.

366 CREIZENACH, Wilhelm. *The English Drama in the Age of Elizabeth.* Philadelphia: Lippincott, 1916.

367 DANBY, John F. *Poets on Fortune's Hill: Studies in Sidney, Shakespeare, Beaumont and Fletcher.* London: Faber and Faber, 1952.

368 DESSEN, Alan C. "The Morall as an Elizabethan Dramatic Kind: An Exploratory Essay." *CompD,* 5 (1971), 138–59.

369 DORAN, Madeleine. *Endeavors of Art: A Study of Form in Elizabethan Drama.* University of Wisconsin Press, 1954.

370 DOWNER, Alan S. *The British Drama.* New York: Appleton-Century-Crofts, 1950.

371 ECKHARDT, Eduard. *Das englischen Drama der Spätrenaissance.* Berlin: de Gruyter, 1929.

372 ECKHARDT, Eduard. *Das englischen Drama im Zeitalter der Reformation und der Hochrenaissance.* Berlin: de Gruyter, 1928.

373 ELLIOTT, John R., Jr. "The History Play as Drama." *RORD,* 11 (1968), 21–28.

374 ELLIS-FERMOR, Una M. *The Frontiers of Drama.* 3d ed. London: Methuen, 1948.

375 ELLIS-FERMOR, Una M. *The Jacobean Drama.* 3d ed., rev. London: Methuen, 1953.

376 ELLISON, L. M. *The Early Romantic Drama at the English Court.* Chicago: University of Chicago Press, 1917.

377 EMPSON, William. *Some Versions of Pastoral.* London: Chatto & Windus, 1935.

378 FELDMAN, A. Bronson. "Gnaphaeus in England." *MLN,* 67 (1952), 325–28.

379 FENTON, Doris. *The Extra-Dramatic Moment in Elizabethan Plays Before 1616.* Philadelphia: University of Pennsylvania Press, 1930.

380 FERGUSSON, Francis. *The Idea of a Theater.* Princeton: Princeton University Press, 1949.

381 FLETCHER, Angus. *Allegory: The Theory of a Symbolic Mode.* Ithaca, N.Y.: Cornell University Press, 1964.

382 FRASER, Russell A. "Elizabethan Drama and The Art of Abstraction." *CompD,* 2 (1968–69), 73–82.

383 FRIEDENREICH, Kenneth. " 'You Talks Brave and Bold': The Origins of an Elizabethan Stage Convention." *CompD,* 8 (1974), 239–53.

384 FROST, David L. *The School of Shakespeare: The Influence of Shakespeare on English Drama 1600–42.* Cambridge: Cambridge University Press, 1968.

385 GILBERT, Allan H. "Logic in the Elizabethan Drama." *SP,* 32 (1935), 527–45.

386 GREENFIELD, Thelma N. *The Induction in Elizabethan Drama.* Eugene: University of Oregon Press, 1969.

387 GREG, W. W. *Pastoral Poetry and Pastoral Drama.* (1906) Reprinted, New York: Russell & Russell, 1959.

388 GRYLLS, Rosalie Glynn. "Greek and Elizabethan Drama." *Contemporary Review,* 126 (1924), 238–44.

389 GURR, A. J. "Elizabethan Action." *SP,* 63 (1966), 144–56.

390 HARBAGE, Alfred B. *The Cavalier Drama.* New York: Modern Language Association, 1936.

391 HARBAGE, Alfred B. *Shakespeare and the Rival Traditions.* New York: Macmillan, 1952.

392 HARDISON, O. B., Jr. *Christian Rite and Christian Drama in the Middle Ages.* Baltimore: The Johns Hopkins Press, 1965.

393 HARDISON, O. B., Jr. "Three Types of Renaissance Catharsis." *RenD,* n.s. 2 (1969), 3–22.

394 HARRISON, G. B. *Elizabethan Plays and Players.* London: Routledge, 1940.

395 HARRISON, G. B. *The Story of Elizabethan Drama.* Cambridge: Cambridge University Press, 1924.

396 HAWKES, Terence. "Postscript: Theatre Against Shakespeare?" *Elizabethan Theatre I.* Pp. 117–26. **See 282.**

397 HAWKINS, Harriett. *Likenesses of Truth in Elizabethan and Restoration Drama.* Oxford: The Clarendon Press, 1972.

398 HERFORD, C. H. *Studies in the Literary Relations of England and Germany in the Sixteenth Century.* Cambridge: Cambridge University Press, 1886.

399 HERRICK, Marvin T. "The New Drama of the Sixteenth Century." *JEGP,* 54 (1955), 555–77.

400 HERRICK, Marvin T. *Tragicomedy: Its Origin and Development in Italy, France, and England.* Urbana: University of Illinois Press, 1955.

401 HEWITT, Douglas. "The Very Pompes of the Divell—Popular and Folk Elements in Elizabethan and Jacobean Drama." *RES,* 25 (1949), 10–23.

402 HIBBARD, G. R. *Thomas Nashe: A Critical Introduction.* Cambridge: Harvard University Press, 1962.

403 HOLDEN, William P. *Anti-Puritan Satire, 1572–1642.* New Haven: Yale University Press, 1954.

404 HOLMES, Elizabeth. *Aspects of Elizabethan Imagery.* Oxford: Basil Blackwell, 1929.

405 HOMAN, Sidney R., Jr. "The Uses of Silence: The Elizabethan Dumb Show and the Silent Cinema." *CompD,* 2 (1968–69), 213–28.

406 HOSLEY, Richard. "The Formal Influence of Plautus and Terrence." *Elizabethan Theatre* (Stratford). Pp. 131–46. **See 277.**

407 HOTSON, Leslie. *The Commonwealth and Restoration Stage.* Cambridge: Harvard University Press, 1928.

408 HOWARTH, R. G. *Literature of the Theatre: Marlowe to Shirley.* Sydney, Australia: Halstead Press, 1953.

409 HOY, Cyrus. "Artifice and Reality and the Decline of Jacobean Drama." *RORD,* 13–14 (1970–71), 169–80.

410 HOY, Cyrus. "Jacobean Tragedy and the Mannerist Style." *SS,* 26 (1973), 49–68.

411 HOY, Cyrus. "Renaissance and Restoration Dramatic Plotting." *RenD,* 9 (1966), 247–64.

412 HUBBARD, F. G. "A Type of Blank Verse Line Found in the Earlier Elizabethan Drama." *PMLA,* n.s. 25 (1917), 68.

413 HUNTER, G. K. "Henry IV and the Elizabethan Two-Part Play." *RES,* 5 (1954), 236–48.

414 HUNTER, G. K. "Italian Tragicomedy on the English Stage." *RenD,* 6 (1973), 123–48.

415 HUNTER, G. K. "Seneca and the Elizabethans: A Case-study in 'Influence.' " *SS,* 20 (1967), 17–26.

416 HYDE, Mary C. *Playwriting for Elizabethans, 1600–1605.* New York: Columbia University Press, 1949.

417 JACQUOT, Jean, ed. *Dramaturgie et société: Rapports entre l'oeuvre théâtrale et son public au XVI et XVII siècles.* 2 vols. Paris: Centre Nationale de la Recherche Scientifique, 1968.

418 JEFFERY, Violet M. "Italian and English Pastoral Drama of the Renaissance: Source of the *Complaint of the Satyrs against the Nymphes." MLR,* 19 (1924), 56–62.

419 JEFFERY, Violet M. "Italian and English Pastoral Drama of the Renaissance: Sources of David's *Queen's Arcadia* and Randolph's *Amyntas." MLR,* 19 (1924), 435–44.

420 JOHNSON, Robert C. "Audience Involvement in the Tudor Interlude." *TN,* 24 (1970), 101–11.

421 JOHNSON, S. F. "The Tragic Hero in Early Elizabethan Drama." *Studies in the English Renaissance Drama.* Pp. 157–71. **See 270.**

422 JONES, Marion. "The Court and the Dramatists." *The Elizabethan Theatre* (Stratford). Pp. 169–96. **See 277.**

423 JONES, Robert C. "Italian Settings and the 'World' of Elizabethan Tragedy." *SEL,* 10 (1970), 251–68.

424 KERNAN, Alvin. *The Cankered Muse: Satire in the English Renaissance.* New Haven: Yale University Press, 1959.

425 KERNODLE, George R. *From Art to Theatre: Form and Convention in the Renaissance.* Chicago: University of Chicago Press, 1944.

426 KERNODLE, George R. "The Mannerist Stage of Comic Detachment," *Elizabethan Theatre III.* Pp. 119–34. **See 284.**

427 KIRSCH, Arthur C. *Jacobean Dramatic Perspectives.* Charlottesville: University Press of Virginia, 1972.

428 KITTO, H. D. F. *Form and Meaning in Drama.* New York: Barnes & Noble, 1956.

429 KLEIN, David. *The Elizabethan Dramatists as Critics.* New York: Philosophical Library, 1963.

430 KNIGHT, W. Nicholas. "Equity and Mercy in English Law and Drama, 1405–1641." *CompD,* 6 (1972), 51–67.

431 KNIGHTS, L. C. *Drama and Society in the Age of Jonson.* London: Chatto & Windus, 1937.

432 KNIGHTS, L. C. "Education and the Drama in the Age of Shakespeare:" *The Criterion,* 11 (1932), 599–625.

433 KÖKERITZ, Helge. *Shakespeare's Pronunciation.* New Haven: Yale University Press, 1953.

434 KOLIN, Philip C. *The Elizabethan Stage Doctor as a Dramatic Convention.* Elizabethan & Renaissance Studies, 41. Salzburg: Institut für Englische Sprache und Literatur, Universität Salzburg, 1975.

435 KRAMER, J. E. *"Damon and Pithias:* An Apology for Art." *ELH,* 35 (1968), 475–90.

436 LANCASHIRE, Anne. *"The Second Maiden's Tragedy:* A Jacobean Saint's Life." *RES,* 25 (1974), 267–79.

437 LANDA, M. J. *The Jew in Drama.* London: King, 1926.

438 LAVIN, J. A. "The Elizabethan Theatre and the Inductive Method." *In Elizabethan Theatre II.* Pp. 74–86. **See 283.**

439 LAW, Robert Adger. *"A Looking Glasse* and the Scriptures." *UTSE,* 19 (1940), 31–47.

440 LEECH, Clifford. "Catholic and Protestant Drama." *DUJ,* 33 (1941), 171–87.

441 LEECH, Clifford. *The Dramatist's Experience, With Other Essays in Literary Theory.* New York: Barnes & Noble, 1970.

442 LEECH, Clifford. "The Function of Locality in the Plays of Shakespeare and His Contemporaries." In *Elizabethan Theatre I.* Pp. 103–16. **See 282.**

443 LEECH, Clifford. "Love and Escape in Caroline Plays." *DUJ,* n.s. 1 (1940), 131–47.

21

444 LEECH, Clifford. "Three Times Ho and a Brace of Widows: Some Plays for the Private Theatre." In *Elizabethan Theatre III.* Pp. 14–32. **See 284.**

445 LEVER, J. W. *The Tragedy of State.* London: Methuen, 1971.

446 LEVIN, Harry. "The End of Elizabethan Drama." *CompD,* 3 (1969–70), 275–81.

447 LEVIN, Harry. *The Myth of the Golden Age in the Renaissance.* Bloomington: University of Indiana Press, 1969.

448 LEVIN, Harry. "The Shakespearean Overplot." *RenD,* 8 (1965), 63–72.

449 LEVIN, Richard. "The Elizabethan 'Three-Level' Play." *RenD,* n.s. 2 (1969), 23–37.

450 LEVIN, Richard. *The Multiple Plot in English Renaissance Drama.* Chicago: University of Chicago Press, 1971.

451 LEVIN, Richard. "My Theme Can Lick Your Theme." *CE,* 37 (1975), 307–12.

452 LEVIN, Richard. "Some Second Thoughts on Central Themes." *MLR,* 67 (1972), 1–10.

453 LEVIN, Richard. "Thematic Unity and the Homogenization of Character." *MLQ,* 33 (1972), 23–29.

454 LEVIN, Richard. "Third Thoughts on Thematics." *MLR,* 70 (1975), 481–96.

455 LIEVSAY, John L. "Italian *Favole boscarecce* and Jacobean Stage Pastoralism." *Essays on Shakespeare and Elizabethan Drama.* Pp. 317–26. **See 287.**

456 LLOYD, Bertram. "The Authorship of *The Welsh Ambassador.*" *RES,* 21 (1945), 192–201.

457 LONG, John H., ed. *Music in English Renaissance Drama.* Lexington: University of Kentucky Press, 1969.

458 LYMAN, D. B., Jr. "Apocryphal Plays of the University Wits." *English Studies in Honor of James Southall Wilson.* Charlottesville: University Press of Virginia, 1951. Pp. 211–21.

459 McCULLEN, Joseph T., Jr. "The Functions of Songs Aroused by Madness in Elizabethan Drama." *A Tribute to George Coffin Taylor.* Chapel Hill: University of North Carolina Press, 1952. Pp. 185–96.

460 McCULLEN, Joseph T., Jr. "Madness and the Isolation of Characters in Elizabethan and Early Stuart Drama." *SP,* 48 (1951), 206–18.

461 McCULLEN, Joseph T., Jr. "The Use of Parlor and Tavern Games in Elizabethan and Early Stuart Drama." *MLQ,* 14 (1953), 7–14.

462 MacDONALD, J. F. "The Use of Prose in English Drama before Shakespeare." *UTQ,* 2 (1933), 465–81.

463 McINTYRE, Clara F. "The Later Career of the Elizabethan Villain-Hero." *PMLA,* 40 (1925), 874–80.

464 McMAHONE, Amos Philip. "Seven Questions on Aristotelian Definitions of Tragedy and Comedy." *Harvard Studies in Classical Philology,* 40 (1931), 97–198.

465 McMILLIN, Scott. "*The Book of Sir Thomas More:* A Theatrical View." *MP,* 68 (1970), 10–24.

466 McNEIR, Waldo F. "Reconstructing the Conclusion of John of Bordeaux." *PMLA,* 66 (1951), 540–43.

467 MAIN, William. "Dramaturgical Norms in the Elizabethan Repertory." *SP,* 54 (1957), 128–48.

468 MANHEIM, Michael. "The Weak King History Play of the Early 1590's." *RenD,* n.s. 2 (1969), 71–80.

469 MARGESON, J. M. R. "Dramatic Form: The Huntington Plays." *SEL,* 14 (1974), 223–38.

470 MARSDEN, Michael T. "The Otherworld of *Arden of Feversham.*" *SFQ,* 36 (1972), 36–42.

471 MARSHALL, Mary Hatch. "Dramatic Tradition Established by the Liturgical Plays." *PMLA,* 56 (1941), 962–91.

472 MARTIN, Mary Forster. *"If You Know Not Me You Know Nobodie* and *The Famous Historie of Sir Thomas Wyatt."* The Library, n.s. 13 (1932), 272–81.

473 MATTHEWS, Ernst G. "The Murdered Substitute Tale." *MLQ,* 6 (1945), 187–95.

474 MATTHIESSEN, F. O. "Towards Our Understanding of Elizabethan Drama." *SoR,* 4 (1938), 398–428.

475 MAXWELL, Baldwin. "The Attitude toward the Duello in Later Jacobean Drama: A Postscript." *PQ,* 54 (1975), 104–16.

476 MAXWELL, Baldwin. "Notes Toward Dating Fletcher's *Wit Without Money.*" *PQ,* 12 (1933), 327–38.

477 MAXWELL, Baldwin. *Studies in the Shakespeare Apocrypha.* New York: Columbia University Press, 1956.

478 MEADLEY, T. D. "Attack on the Theatre (ca. 1500–1680)." *London Quarterly of Holborn Review* (January, 1953), 36–41.

479 MEHL, Dieter. *The Elizabethan Dumb Show: The History of a Dramatic Convention.* Cambridge: Harvard University Press, 1966.

480 MEHL, Dieter. "Emblems in English Renaissance Drama." *RenD,* n.s. 2 (1969), 39–57.

481 MEHL, Dieter. "Form and Function of the Play Within a Play." *RenD,* 8 (1965), 41–62.

482 MENDELL, Clarence W. *Our Seneca.* New Haven: Yale University Press, 1941.

483 MEYER, Edward. "Machiavelli and the Elizabethan Drama." *Literarhistorische Forschungen,* 1 (1897), 1–180.

484 MINCOFF, M. "The Authorship of *The Two Noble Kinsmen.*" *ES,* 33 (1952), 97–115.

485 MOORE, John Robert. "The Tradition of Angelic Singing in English Drama." *JEGP,* 22 (1923), 89–99.

486 MOTTER, T. H. V. *The School Drama in England.* London: Longman's, 1929.

487 MULLANY, Peter F. "The Knights of Malta in Renaissance Drama." *Neuphilologische Mitteilungen,* 74 (1973), 297–310.

488 MYERS, Aaron Michael. *Representation and Misrepresentation of the Puritan in Elizabethan Drama.* Philadelphia: University of Pennsylvania Press, 1931.

489 NICOLL, Allardyce. *British Drama.* Rev. ed. New York: Crowell, 1933.

490 NICOLL, Allardyce. *The Development of the Theatre.* 4th ed., rev. New York: Harcourt, Brace, 1958.

491 NICOLL, Allardyce. *An Introduction to Dramatic Theory.* London: Harrap, 1923.

492 NICOLL, Allardyce. " 'Tragical—Comical—Historical—Pastoral': Elizabethan Dramatic Nomenclature." *BJRL,* 43 (1960), 70–87.

493 OLIPHANT, E. H. C. "Collaboration in Elizabethan Drama: Mr. W. J. Lawrence's Theory." *PQ,* 8 (1929), 1–10.

494 OLIVER, H. J. "Literary Allusions in Jacobean Drama." *Renaissance Studies in Honor of Carroll Camden.* Pp. 131–140. **See 291.**

495 ORGEL, Stephen. *The Illusion of Power: Political Theater in the English Renaissance.* Berkeley: University of California Press, 1975.

496 ORR, David. *Italian Renaissance Drama in England before 1625.* Chapel Hill: University of North Carolina Press, 1970.

497 ORSINI, Napoleone. "Caratteri estetici del drama elisabettiano." *Anglica,* II, 2 (1948), 1–19.

498 ORSINI, Napoleone. " 'Policy' Or the Language of Elizabethan Machiavellianism." *JWCI,* 9 (1946), 122–34.

499 PALMER, D. J. "Elizabethan Tragic Heroes." In *Elizabethan Theatre* (Stratford). Pp. 11–37. **See 277.**

500 PARKES, H. B. "Nature's Diverse Laws: The Double Vision of the Elizabethans." *SR,* 58 (1950), 402–18.

501 PARROTT, T. M., and Robert H. BALL. *A Short View of Elizabethan Drama.* New York: Scribners, 1943.

502 PASACHOFF, Naomi E. *Playwrights, Preachers, and Politicians: A Study of Four Tudor Old Testament Dramas.* Elizabethan & Renaissance Studies 45. Salzburg: Institut für Englische Sprache und Literatur, Universität Salzburg, 1975.

503 PEARN, B. R. "Dumb-show in Elizabethan Drama." *RES,* 11 (1935), 385–405.

504 PENNIMAN, Josiah H. *The War of the Theatres.* Philadelphia: University of Pennsylvania Press, 1897.

505 PETER, John. *Complaint and Satire in Early English Literature.* Oxford: The Clarendon Press, 1956.

506 PRAZ, Mario. "Machiavelli and the Elizabethans." *Proceedings of the British Academy,* 14 (1928), 49–97. Reprinted with revisions in *The Flaming Heart.* New York: Doubleday, 1958. Pp. 90–145.

507 PRESSON, Robert K. "Two Types of Dreams in the Elizabethan Drama, and Their Heritage: *Somnium Animale* and the Prick-of-Conscience." *SEL,* 7 (1967), 239–56.

508 PRICE, George R. "The Authorship and the Manuscript of *The Old Law.*" *HLQ,* 16 (1953), 117–139.

509 PUTT, S. Gorley. "An Argumentative Muse. A Background for the 'University Wits'." In *E&S 1972* (1973), 45–56.

510 PUTT, S. Gorley. "The Relevance of Jacobean Drama." *E&S* (1970), 18–33.

511 RABKIN, Norman. "The Double Plot: Notes on the History of a Convention." *RenD,* 7 (1964), 55–69.

512 RABKIN, Norman, ed. *Reinterpretations of Elizabethan Drama.* English Institute Papers. New York: Columbia University Press, 1969.

513 RANSOM, Harry. "Some Legal Elements in Elizabethan Plays." *UTSE,* 16 (1936), 53–76.

514 REBORA, P. *L'Italia nel dramma inglese (1558–1642).* London: Truslove & Hanson, 1925.

515 REED, Robert R., Jr. *Bedlam on the Jacobean Stage.* Cambridge: Harvard University Press, 1952.

516 REIBETANZ, John. "Hieronimo in Decimosexto: A Private-Theater Burlesque." *RenD,* 5 (1972), 89–121.

517 REYBURN, Marjorie L. "New Facts and Theories about the Parnassus Plays." *PMLA,* 74 (1959), 325–35.

518 REYNOLDS, George F. "Aims of a Popular Elizabethan Dramatist." *PQ,* 20 (1941), 340–4.

519 RICKS, Christopher. *English Drama to 1710.* History of Literature in the English Language, III. London: Sphere, Barrie & Jenkins, 1971.

520 RIGHTER, Anne. *Shakespeare and the Idea of the Play.* London: Chatto & Windus, 1962.

521 RISTINE, Frank Humphrey. *English Tragicomedy: Its Origin and History.* New York: Columbia University Press, 1910.

522 ROSS, Lawrence J. "Art and the Study of Early English Drama." *RenD,* 6 (1963), 35–46.

523 ROSSITER, A. P. *English Drama from Early Times to the Elizabethans.* London: Hutchinson, 1950; 2d ed., 1969.

523A ROSTON, Murray. *Biblical Drama in English: From the Middle Ages to the Present Day.* London: Faber, 1968.

524 RUSSELL, H. K. "Elizabethan Dramatic Poetry in the Light of Natural and Moral Philosophy." *PQ,* 12 (1933), 187–95.

525 RUSSELL, Patricia. "Romantic Narrative Plays: 1570–1590." *Elizabethan Theatre* (Stratford). Pp. 107–30. **See 277.**

526 SACKTON, Alexander H. "The Paradoxical Encomium in Elizabethan Drama." *UTSE,* 28 (1949), 83–104.

527 SALESKI, R. E. "Supernatural Agents in Christian Imagery: Word Studies in Elizabethan Dramatists." *JEGP,* 38 (1939), 431–39.

528 SALINGAR, Leo G. *Shakespeare and the Traditions of Comedy.* London: Cambridge University Press, 1974.

529 SALOMON, Brownell. "Visual and Aural Signs in The Performed English Renaissance Play." *RenD,* n.s. 5 (1972), 143–69.

530 SANVIC, Romain. *Le Théâtre élizabéthain.* Brussels: Office de Publiçité, 1955.

531 SCHELLING, F. E. *Elizabethan Playwrights: A Short History of the English Drama from Medieval Times to the Closing of the Theatres in 1642.* New York: Harper, 1925.

532 SCHELLING, F. E. *Foreign Influences in Elizabethan Plays.* New York: Harper, 1923.

533 SCHOECK, R. J. "Early Tudor Drama and the Inns of Court." *American Society for Theatre Research Newsletter,* 2 (1957), 6–10.

534 SCHOENBAUM, S. "Internal Evidence and the Attribution of Elizabethan Plays." *BNYPL,* 65 (1961), 102–24.

535 SCHOENBAUM, S. *Internal Evidence and Elizabethan Dramatic Authorship.* Evanston, Ill.: Northwestern University Press, 1966.

536 SEMPER, I. J. "The Jacobean Theatre Through the Eyes of Catholic Clerics." *SQ,* 3 (1952), 45–51.

537 SENSABAUGH, G. F. "Love Ethics in Platonic Court Drama 1625–1642." *HLB,* 1 (1938), 277–304.

538 SHARPE, Robert B. *Irony in the Drama.* Chapel Hill: University of North Carolina Press, 1959.

539 SHARPE, Robert B. "Metaphysical Paradox in Jacobean Drama." *RenP 1960,* (1961), 19–23.

540 SHAW, Phillip. "Sir Thomas Wyatt and the Scenario of *Lady Jane.*" *MLQ,* 13 (1952), 227–38.

541 SHERBO, Arthur. "The Knight of Malta and Boccaccio's *Filocolo.*" *ES,* 33 (1952), 254–97.

542 SIBLY, John. "The Duty of Revenge in Tudor and Stuart Drama." *REL,* 8 (1967), 46–54.

543 SIMEONE, William E. "Renaissance Robin Hood Plays." *Folklore in Action: Essays for Discussion in Honor of MacEdward Leach.* Horace P. Beck, ed. Philadelphia: American Folklore Society, 1962.

544 SIMPSON, Percy. *Studies in Elizabethan Drama.* Oxford: The Clarendon Press, 1955.

545 SISSON, C. J. *The Elizabethan Dramatists except Shakespeare.* London: Benn, 1928.

546 SISSON, C. J. and Arthur BROWN. " 'The Great Danseker': Literary Significance of a Chancery Suit." *MLR,* 46 (1951), 339–48.

547 SMITH, Bruce R. "Sir Amorous Knight and the Indecorous Romans; or, Plautus and Terence Play Court in the Renaissance," *RenD,* 6 (1973), 3–27.

548 SMITH, G. C. Moore. *College Plays Performed in the University of Cambridge.* Cambridge: Cambridge University Press, 1923.

549 SOELLNER, Rolf. "The Madness of Hercules and the Elizabethans." *CL,* 10 (1958), 309–24.

550 SPEAIGHT, Robert. *William Poel and the Elizabethan Revival.* London: Heinemann, 1954.

551 SPENCER, Theodore. "The Elizabethan Malcontent." *Joseph Quincy Adams Memorial Studies.* Pp. 523–35. **See 289.**

552 STAMM, Rudolf. *Geschichte des englischen Theaters.* Bern: A Franche, 1951.

553 STEADMAN, John M. "Iconography and Methodology in Renaissance Dramatic Study: Some Caveats." *SRO,* 7–8 (1972–74), 39–52.

554 STEADMAN, John M. "Iconography and Renaissance Drama: Ethical and Mythological Themes." *RORD,* 13–14 (1970–71), 73–122.

555 STERN, Charlotte. "The Early Spanish Drama: From Medieval Ritual to Renaissance Art." *RenD,* 6 (1973), 177–201.

556 STEVENSON, Hazel Allison. "The Major Elizabethan Poets and the Doctrine of Signatures." *Florida State University Studies,* 5 (1952), 11–31.

557 STOLL, E. E. "The Tragic Fallacy, So-Called." *UTQ,* 5 (1936), 457–81.

558 STONEX, Arthur B. "The Usurer in Elizabethan Drama." *PMLA,* 31 (1916), 190–210.

559 STROUP, Thomas B. *Microcosmos: The Shape of the Elizabethan Play.* Lexington: University of Kentucky Press, 1965.

560 SYKES, H. Dugdale. *Sidelights on Elizabethan Drama.* Oxford: The Clarendon Press, 1924.

561 SYMONDS, J. A. *Shakespere's Predecessors in the English Drama.* London: Smith, Elder, 1884.

562 SYPHER, Wylie. *Four Stages of Renaissance Style.* Garden City, N.Y.: Doubleday, 1955.

563 TALBERT, Ernest W. *Elizabethan Drama and Shakespeare's Early Plays.* Chapel Hill: University of North Carolina Press, 1963.

564 THALER, Alwin. *Shakspere to Sheridan.* Cambridge: Harvard University Press, 1922.

565 THORP, Willard. *The Triumph of Realism in Elizabethan Drama 1558–1612.* Princeton: Princeton University Press, 1928.

566 TUPPER, Frederick. "The Envy Theme in Prologues and Epilogues." *JEGP,* 16 (1917), 551.

567 TURNER, Robert K., Jr. "Act-End Notations of Some Elizabethan Plays." *MP,* 72 (1975), 238–47.

568 TURNER, Robert Y. "The Causal Induction in Some Elizabethan Plays." *SP,* 60 (1963), 183–90.

569 URE, Peter. "The 'Deformed Mistress' Theme and the Platonic Convention." *N&Q,* 193 (1948), 269–70.

570 URE, Peter. *Elizabethan and Jacobean Drama: Critical Essays.* English Text & Studies Series. Maxwell, J. C. New York: Barnes & Noble, 1974.

571 VAN DER SPEK, C. *The Church and the Churchman in English Dramatic Literature before 1642.* Amsterdam: H. J. Paris, 1930.

572 VANDIVER, E. P., Jr. "The Elizabethan Dramatic Parasite." *SP,* 32 (1935), 411–27.

573 WAITH, Eugene M. *Ideas of Greatness: Heroic Drama in England.* London: Routledge & Kegan Paul, 1971.

574 WEBBER, Edwin J. "On the Ancestry of The Gracioso." *RenD,* n.s. 5 (1972), 171–90.

575 WELLS, Henry W. *Elizabethan and Jacobean Playwrights.* New York: Columbia University Press, 1939.

576 WELSFORD, Enid. *The Fool: His Social and Literary History.* London: Faber & Faber, 1935.

577 WEST, Robert H. *The Invisible World: A Study in Pneumatology in Elizabethan Drama.* Athens: University of Georgia Press, 1939.

578 WHITING, B. J. *Proverbs in the Earlier English Drama.* Cambridge: Harvard University Press, 1938.

579 WICKHAM, Glynne. "The Privy Council Order of 1597 for the Destruction of All London's Theatres." *Elizabethan Theatre I.* Pp. 21–44. See 282.

580 WICKHAM, Glynne. *Shakespeare's Dramatic Heritage.* New York: Barnes & Noble, 1969.

581 WIERUM, Ann. " 'Actors' and 'Play-Acting' in the Morality Tradition." *RenD,* n.s. 3 (1970), 189–214.

582 WILEY, A. N. "Female Prologues and Epilogues in English Plays." *PMLA,* 48 (1933), 1060–79.

583 WILLIAMS, Raymond. *Drama in Performance.* Baltimore: Penguin, 1973.

584 WILLIAMSON, George. "Elizabethan Drama and its Classical Rival." *University of California Chronicles,* 31 (1929), 251–6.

585 WILSON, Edward M. "Family Honour in the Plays of Shakespeare's Predecessors and Contemporaries." *E&S 1953,* 19–40.

586 WILSON, F. P. *Elizabethan and Jacobean.* Oxford: The Clarendon Press, 1945.

587 WILSON, F. P. *The English Drama: 1485–1585.* New York: Oxford University Press, 1969.

588 WITHINGTON, Robert. *Excursions in English Drama.* New York: Appleton Century, 1937.

589 WOLFF, M. J. "Die soziale Stellung der englischen Renaissancedramatiker." *Englische Studien,* 71 (1937), 179–90.

590 WOLFF, M. J. "Zum englischen Renaissancedrama." *Germanischromanische Monatsschrift,* 17 (1929), 295–302.

591 WRIGHT, Louis B. "The Scriptures and the Elizabethan Stage." *MP,* 26 (1928), 47–56.

592 WRIGHT, Louis B. and Virginia LaMAR. *Life and Letters in Tudor and Stuart England.* Ithaca: Cornell University Press, 1962.

593 YATES, Frances A. *Theatre of the World.* London: Routledge & Kegan Paul, 1969.

594 YOUNG, Steven C. *The Frame Structure in Tudor and Stuart Drama.* Elizabethan and Renaissance Studies 6. Salzburg: Institut für Englische Sprache und Literatur, Universität Salzburg, 1974.

Moralities and Interludes

595 ADAMS, Barry B., ed. *John Bale's "King Johan."* San Marino, Calif.: The Huntington Library, 1969.

596 BERNARD, J. E., Jr. *The Prosody of the Tudor Interlude.* New Haven: Yale University Press, 1939.

597 BEVINGTON, David M. *From Mankind to Marlowe: Growth of Structure in the Popular Drama of Tudor England.* Cambridge: Harvard University Press, 1962.

598 BLATT, Thora Balslev. *The Plays of John Bale: A Study of Ideas, Technique and Style.* Copenhagen: Gad, 1968.

599 CARPENTER, Nan Cooke. *John Skelton.* New York: Twayne, 1967.

600 CRAIG, Hardin. *English Religious Drama of the Middle Ages.* Oxford: The Clarendon Press, 1955.

601 CRAIG, Hardin. "Morality Plays and Elizabethan Drama." *SQ,* 1 (1950), 64–72.

602 CRAIK, T. W. *The Tudor Interlude: Stage, Costume, and Acting.* Leicester: Leicester University Press, 1958.

603 CRAIK, T. W. "The Tudor Interlude and Later Elizabethan Drama." *Elizabethan Theatre* (Stratford). Pp. 37–58. **See 277.**

604 CUSHMAN, L. W. *The Devil and the Vice in the English Dramatic Literature Before Shakespeare.* Halle: M. Niemeyer, 1910.

605 DESSEN, Alan. "The 'Estates' Morality Play." *SP,* 62 (1965), 121–36.

606 GARDINER, H. C. *Mysteries End: An Investigation of the Last Days of the Medieval Religious Stage.* New Haven: Yale University Press, 1946.

607 HABICHT, Werner. "The *Wit*-Interludes and the Form of Pre-Shakespearean 'Romantic Comedy.' " *RenD,* 8 (1965), 73–88.

608 HARRIS, William O. *Skelton's "Magnyfycence" and the Cardinal Virtue Tradition.* Durham: University of North Carolina Press, 1965.

609 HOGREFE, Pearl. *The Sir Thomas More Circle: A Program of Ideas and Their Impact on Secular Drama.* Urbana: University of Illinois Press, 1959.

610 HOULE, Peter J. *The English Morality and Related Drama.* Hamden, Conn.: Archon, 1973.

611 INGRAM, R. W. "*Gammer Gurton's Needle:* Comedy Not Quite of the Lowest Order?" *SEL,* 7 (1967), 257–68.

612 JOHNSON, Robert C. "Stage Directions in the Tudor Interlude." *TN,* 26 (1971), 36–42.

613 JONES, Robert C. "Dangerous Sport: The Audience's Engagement with Vice in the Moral Interludes." *RenD,* 6 (1973), 45–64.

614 JONES, Robert C. "The Stage World and the 'Real' World in Medwall's *Fulgens and Lucrece.*" *MLQ,* 32 (1971), 131–42.

615 KINSMAN, Robert S. "Skelton's *Magnyfycence:* The Strategy of the 'Olde Sayde Sawe.' " *SP,* 63 (1966), 99–125.

616 LENNAM, Trevor. *Sebastian Westcott, the Children of Paul's, and "The Marriage of Wit and Science."* Toronto: University of Toronto Press, 1975.

617 McCUTCHAN, J. Wilson. "Justice and Equity in the English Morality Play." *JHI,* 19 (1958), 405–10.

618 MACKENZIE, W. R. *The English Moralities from the Point of View of Allegory.* Boston: Houghton Mifflin, 1914.

619 MARES, Francis Hugh. "The Origin of the Figure Called 'the Vice' in Tudor Drama." *HLQ,* 22 (1958), 11–29.

620 MYERS, James P., Jr. "The Heart of King Cambises." *SP,* 70 (1973), 367–76.

621 NICOLL, Allardyce. *The World of Harlequin.* New York: Cambridge University Press, 1963.

622 OWST, G. R. *Literature and Pulpit in Medieval England.* 2d ed., rev. New York: Barnes & Noble, 1961.

623 PINEAS, Rainer. "The English Morality Play as a Weapon of Religious Controversy." *SEL,* 2 (1962), 157–80.

624 REED, Arthur W. *The Beginnings of the English Secular and Romantic Drama.* Shakespeare Association Pamphlet. Oxford: Oxford University Press, 1922.

625 REED, Arthur W. *Early Tudor Drama.* London: Methuen, 1926.

626 SPIVACK, Bernard. *Shakespeare and the Allegory of Evil.* New York: Columbia University Press, 1958.

627 THOMPSON, Elbert N. S. *The English Moral Play.* New Haven: Connecticutt Academy of Arts, Science and Letters, 1910.

628 VELZ, John W., and Carl P. DAW, Jr. "Tradition and Originality in *Wyt and Science.*" *SP,* 65 (1968), 631–46.

629 WRIGHT, Louis B. "Social Aspects of Some Belated Moralities." *Anglia,* 54 (1930), 107–48.

Comedy

630 ARMIN, Robert. *The Collected Works of Robert Armin.* J. P. Feather, ed. 2 vols. New York & London: Johnson Reprint, 1972.

631 BECK, Ervin. "Terence Improved: The Paradigm of the Prodigal Son in English Renaissance Comedy." *RenD,* 6 (1973), 107–22.

632 BLISTEIN, Elmer M. *Comedy in Action:* Durham, N.C.: Duke University Press, 1964.

633 BOUGHNER, Daniel C. *The Braggart in Renaissance Comedy.* Minneapolis: University of Minnesota Press, 1954.

634 BOURGY, V. *Le Bouffon sur la scène anglaise au XVI siècle.* Paris: Les Editions de l'office Central de Librarie, 1970.

635 BRADBROOK, M. C. "The Comedy of Timon." *RenD,* 9 (1966), 83–103.

636 BRADBROOK, M. C. *The Growth and Structure of Elizabethan Comedy.* London: Chatto & Windus, 1955.

637 BROWN, Arthur. "Citizen Comedy and Domestic Drama," in *Jacobean Theatre.* Pp. 63–84. **See 276.**

638 CURRY, John V. *Deception in Elizabethan Comedy.* Chicago: Loyola University Press, 1955.

639 FARNHAM, Willard. "Mediaeval Comic Spirit in the English Renaissance." *Joseph Quincy Adams Memorial Studies.* Pp. 429–37. **See 289.**

640 FELDMAN, Sylvia D. *The Morality-Patterned Comedy of the Renaissance.* The Hague: Mouton, 1970.

641 FELVER, Charles S. "The *Commedia dell'Arte* and English Drama in the Sixteenth and Early Seventeenth Centuries." *RenD,* 6 (1963), 24–34.

642 GIBBONS, Brian. *Jacobean City Comedy: A Study of Satiric Plays by Jonson, Marston and Middleton.* Cambridge: Harvard University Press, 1968.

643 HERRICK, Marvin T. *Comic Theory in the Sixteenth Century.* Urbana: University of Illinois Press, 1950.

644 HERRICK, Marvin T. *Italian Comedy in the Renaissance.* Urbana: University of Illinois Press, 1960.

645 HORWICH, Richard. "Wives, Courtesans, and the Economics of Love in Jacobean City Comedy." *CompD,* 7 (1973–74), 291–309.

646 JENSEN, Ejner. "The Changing Faces of Love in English Renaissance Comedy." *CompD,* 6 (1972–73), 294–309.

647 KAPLAN, Joel H. "The Medieval Origins of Elizabethan Comedy: Review Article." *RenD,* 5 (1972), 225–36.

648 KAUFMAN, Helen. "The Influence of Italian Drama on Pre-Restoration English Comedy." *Italica,* 31 (1954), 9–23.

649 KERNAN, Alvin. *The Cankered Muse: Satire of the English Renaissance.* New Haven: Yale University Press, 1959.

650 KRONENBERGER, Louis. *The Thread of Laughter: Chapters on English Stage Comedy from Jonson to Maugham.* New York: Knopf, 1952.

651 LEA, Kathleen M. *Italian Popular Comedy,* 2 vols. (1934) Reprinted, New York: Russell & Russell, 1962.

652 LEGGATT, Alexander. *Citizen Comedy in the Age of Shakespeare.* Toronto: University of Toronto Press, 1973.

653 McKERROW, R. B., ed. *The Works of Thomas Nashe* 5 vols. (1904). Reprinted, Oxford: Blackwell, 1958.

654 PERRY, Henry Ten Eyck. *Masters of Dramatic Comedy and Their Social Themes.* Cambridge: Harvard University Press, 1940.

655 POTTS, L. J. *Comedy.* London and New York: Hutchinson's University Library, 1948.

656 REIBETANZ, John. "Hieronimo in Decimosexto: A Private-Theater Burlesque." *RenD,* n.s. 5 (1972), 89–122.

657 SOMERSET, J. A. B. " 'Fair is foul and foul is fair': Vice-Comedy's Development and Theatrical Effects." *The Elizabethan Theatre V.* Pp. 54–75. **See 286.**

658 SWAIN, Barbara. *Fools and Folly During the Middle Ages and the Renaissance.* New York: Columbia University Press, 1932.

659 THORNDIKE, Ashley H. *English Comedy.* New York: Macmillan, 1929.

660 TOOLE, William B., III. "The Aesthetics of Scatology in *Gammer Gurton's Needle.*" *ELN,* 10 (1973), 252–8.

661 WELD, John S. *Meaning in Comedy: Studies in Elizabethan Romantic Comedy.* Albany: State University of New York Press, 1975.

662 WILLEFORD, William. *The Fool and His Scepter.* Evanston, Ill.: Northwestern University Press, 1969.

663 WINSLOW, Ola Elizabeth. *Low Comedy as a Structural Element in English Drama from the Beginnings to 1642.* Chicago: Distributed by the University of Chicago Libraries, 1926.

664 WRIGHT, Louis B. "Variety-Show Clownery on the Pre-Restoration Stage." *Anglia,* 52 (1928), 51–68.

Tragedy

665 ADAMS, H. H. *English Domestic or Homiletic Tragedy.* New York: Columbia University Press, 1943.

666 ANDERSON, Ruth L. "Excessive Goodness a Tragic Fault." *SAB,* 19 (1944), 85–66.

666 ANDERSON, Ruth L. "Excessive Goodness a Tragic Fault." *SAB,* 19 (1944), 85–96.

667 BABULA, William. "*Gorboduc* as Apology and Critique." *TSL,* 17 (1972), 37–43.

668 BACQUET, Paul. *Un Contemporain d'Elizabeth I: Thomas Sackville, l'homme et l'oeuvre.* Geneva: Droz: 1966.

669 BAKER, Howard. *Induction to Tragedy.* Baton Rouge: Louisiana State University Press, 1939.

670 BECKINGHAM, C. F. "Seneca's Fatalism and Elizabethan Tragedy." *MLR,* 32 (1937), 434–8.

671 BOWERS, Fredson T. "The Audience and the Poisoners of Elizabethan Tragedy." *JEGP,* 36 (1937), 491–504.

672 BOWERS, Fredson T. *Elizabethan Revenge Tragedy: 1587–1642.* Princeton: Princeton University Press, 1940.

673 BOYER, Clarence V. *The Villain as Hero in Elizabethan Tragedy.* London, 1916. Reprinted, New York: Russell & Russell, 1964.

674 BRADBROOK, M. C. *Themes and Conventions of Elizabethan Tragedy.* Cambridge: Cambridge University Press, 1935.

675 BRODWIN, Leonora L. *Elizabethan Love Tragedy, 1587–1625.* New York: New York University Press, 1971.

676 BROUDE, Ronald. "Revenge and Revenge Tragedy in Renaissance England." *RenQ,* 28 (1975), 38–58.

677 BROUDE, Ronald. "*Vindicta Filia Temporis:* Three English Forerunners of the Elizabethan Revenge Play." *JEGP,* 72 (1971), 489–502.

678 CALDWELL, H. B. and D. L. MIDDLETON, comps. *English Tragedy, 1370–1600: Fifty Years of Criticism.* San Antonio, Tex.: Trinity University Press, 1971.

679 CAMPBELL, Lily B. "Theories of Revenge in Renaissance England." *MP,* 28 (1931), 281–96.

680 CHAMARD, Henri. *La Tragédie de la Renaissance.* Cours professé à la faculté des lettres de Paris, 1–5. Paris: R. Guillon, 1929.

681 CHARLTON, H. B. *The Senecan Tradition in Renaissance Tragedy.* Manchester: University of Manchester Press, 1946.

682 CLAY, Charlotte N. *The Role of Anxiety in English Tragedy: 1580–1642.* Jacobean Drama Studies. Salzburg: Institut für Englische Sprache und Literatur, Universität Salzburg, 1974.

683 CLEMEN, Wolfgang. *English Tragedy Before Shakespeare.* T. S. Dorsch, trans. London: Methuen, 1961.

CRITICAL AND HISTORICAL STUDIES

684 COLE, Douglas. "The Comic Accomplice in Elizabethan Revenge Tragedy." *RenD,* 9 (1966), 125–39.

685 CRAIG, Hardin. "The Shackling of Accidents: A Study of Elizabethan Tragedy." *PQ,* 19 (1940), 1–19.

686 CUNLIFFE, John W. *The Influence of Seneca on Elizabethan Tragedy.* London: Macmillan, 1893. Reprinted, New York: G. E. Stechert, 1907.

687 DIXON, W. Macneile. *Tragedy.* London: Edward Arnold, 1924.

688 FANSLER, Harriott E. *The Evolution of Technic in Elizabethan Tragedy.* Chicago: Row, Peterson, 1914.

689 FARNHAM, Willard. *The Medieval Heritage of Elizabethan Tragedy.* Berkeley: University of California Press, 1936. Rev. ed. Oxford: Blackwell 1956.

690 FARNHAM, Willard. "The 'Mirror for Magistrates' and Elizabethan Tragedy." *JEGP,* 25 (1926), 66–78.

691 FRYE, Northrop. "The Mythos of Autumn: Tragedy." *Anatomy of Criticism.* Princeton: Princeton University Press, 1957. Pp. 206–23.

692 FUZIER, Jean. "La Tragédie de vengeance Elisabéthaine et le théâtre dans le théâtre." *RSH,* 145 (1972), 17–33.

693 GARDNER, Helen. "Milton's and the Theme of Damnation in Elizabethan Tragedy." *E&S 1948,* 46–66.

694 HARBAGE, Alfred B. "Intrigue in Elizabethan Tragedy." *Essays on Shakespeare and Elizabethan Drama.* Pp. 37–44. See 287.

695 HENN, T. R. *The Harvest of Tragedy.* London: Methuen, 1956.

696 HERNDL, George C. *The High Design: English Renaissance Tragedy and the Natural Law.* Lexington: University Press of Kentucky, 1970.

697 HIBBARD, G. R. "The Early Seventeenth Century and the Tragic View of Life." *RMS,* 5 (1961), 101–15.

698 HOY, Cyrus. Jacobean Tragedy and the Mannerist Style." *SS,* 26 (1973), 49–67.

699 JEPSEN, Laura. *Ethical Aspects of Tragedy.* Gainesville: University of Florida Press, 1953.

700 JOHNSON, S. F. "The Tragic Hero in Early Elizabethan Drama." *Studies in the English Renaissance Drama.* Pp. 157–71. See 270.

701 LEECH, Clifford. "The Implications of Tragedy." *English,* 6 (1947), 177–82.

702 LEECH, Clifford. "The Incredible in Jacobean Tragedy." *Renaissance Studies in Honor of Carroll Camden.* Pp. 109–22. See 291.

703 LEECH, Clifford. *Shakespeare's Tragedies and Other Studies in Seventeenth-Century Drama.* London: Chatto & Windus, 1950.

704 LEVER, J. W. *The Tragedy of State.* London: Methuen, 1971.

705 LUCAS, F. L. *Seneca and Elizabethan Tragedy.* Cambridge: Cambridge University Press, 1922.

706 McDIARMID, M. P. "The Influence of Robert Garnier on Some Elizabethan Tragedies." *EA,* 11 (1958), 289–302.

707 McDONALD, Charles O. *The Rhetoric of Tragedy: Form in Stuart Drama.* Amherst: University of Massachusetts Press, 1968.

33

708 MARGESON, J. M. R. *The Origins of English Tragedy.* Oxford: The Clarendon Press, 1967.

709 MASON, E. C. "Satire on Women and Sex in Elizabethan Tragedy." *ES,* 31 (1950), 1–10.

710 MICHEL, Laurence. "Yardsticks for Tragedy." *EIC,* 5 (1955), 81–8.

711 MORRISON, Mary. "Some Aspects of the Treatment of the Theme of Antony and Cleopatra in the Tragedies of the Sixteenth Century," *JES,* 4 (1974), 113–25.

712 OLSON, Elder. *Tragedy and the Theory of Drama.* Detroit: Wayne State University Press, 1961.

713 ORNSTEIN, Robert. *The Moral Vision of Jacobean Tragedy.* Madison: University of Wisconsin Press, 1960.

714 PALMER, D. J. "Elizabethan Tragic Heroes." *Elizabethan Theatre* (Stratford). Pp. 11–36. See 277.

715 PRIOR, Moody E. *The Language of Tragedy.* New York: Columbia University Press, 1947.

716 PUTT, S. Gorley. '*Ginger hot i' the mouth':* The Realistic Impact of Jacobean Tragedy. Exeter: University of Exeter, 1975.

717 RIBNER, Irving. *Jacobean Tragedy: The Quest for Moral Order.* London: Methuen, 1962.

718 ROBERTS, Preston. "A Christian Theory of Dramatic Tragedy." *Journal of Religion,* 31 (1951), 1–20.

719 ROHRBERGER, Mary, and Dorothy H. PETTY. "The English Folk-Hero and Elizabethan Tragedy." *Journal of Popular Culture,* 9 (1975), 629–37.

720 ROLLE, Dietrich. *Ingenious Structure: Die dramatisch Funktion der Sprache in der Tragödie der Shakespearezeit. Anglistische Forschungen* (Heidelberg), 99 (1971).

721 SCHÜCKING, Levin L. *The Baroque Character of the Elizabethan Tragic Hero.* London: Oxford University Press, 1938.

722 SEWALL, Richard B. *The Vision of Tragedy.* New Haven: Yale University Press, 1959.

723 SIBLY, John. "The Duty of Revenge in Tudor and Stuart Drama." *REL,* 8 (1967), 46–54.

724 SIMPSON, Percy. "The Theme of Revenge in Elizabethan Tragedy." *Studies in Elizabethan Drama.* Oxford: The Clarendon Press, 1955. Pp. 138–78.

725 SPENCER, Theodore. *Death and Elizabethan Tragedy.* Cambridge: Harvard University Press, 1936.

726 STODDER, Joseph Henry. *Satire in Jacobean Tragedy.* Jacobean Drama Studies 35. Salzburg: Institut für Englische Sprache und Literatur, Universität Salzburg, 1974.

727 STROUP, Thomas B. "The Testing Pattern in Elizabethan Tragedy." *SEL,* 3 (1963), 175–90.

728 STROZIER, Robert M. "Politics, Stoicism, and the Development of Elizabethan Tragedy." *Costerus,* 8 (1973), 193–218.

729 TOMLINSON, T. B. *A Study of Elizabethan and Jacobean Tragedy.* London: Cambridge University Press, 1964.

730 URE, Peter. "On Some Differences between Senecan and Elizabethan Tragedy." *DUJ*, 10 (1948), 17–23.

731 WEISINGER, Herbert. *Tragedy and the Paradox of the Fortunate Fall.* East Lansing: Michigan State College Press, 1953.

732 WELLS, Henry W. "Senecan Influence on Elizabethan Tragedy: A Re-Estimation." *SAB*, 19 (1944), 71–84.

733 WHITMORE, C. E. *The Supernatural in Tragedy.* Cambridge: Harvard University Press, 1915.

734 WITHERSPOON, Alexander M. *The Influence of Robert Garnier on Elizabethan Drama.* New Haven: Yale University Press, 1924.

735 WOOLF, Rosemary. "The Influence of the Mystery Plays upon the Popular Tragedies of the 1560's" *RenD,* (1973), 89–105.

The History Play

735A ANDERSON, Ruth L. "Kingship in Renaissance Drama." *SP*, 41 (1949), 136–55.

736 BERGERON, David M. "Civic Pageants and Historical Drama." *JMRS,* 5 (1975), 89–105.

737 CRAIG, Hardin. "The Origin of the History Play." *Arlington Quarterly,* 1 (1968), 5–11.

738 DRIVER, T. F. *The Sense of History in Greek and Shakespearean Drama.* New York: Columbia University Press, 1960.

739 FLEISCHER, Martha Hester. *The Iconography of the English History Play.* Elizabethan & Renaissance Studies 10. Salzburg: Institut für Englische Sprache und Literatur, Universität Salzburg, 1974.

740 LINDABURY, R. B. *A Study of Patriotism in the Elizabethan Drama.* Princeton: Princeton University Press, 1931.

741 MANHEIM, Michael. "The Weak King History Play of the Early 1590's." *RenD,* n.s. 2 (1969), 71–80.

742 REESE, Gertrude C. "The Question of the Succession in Elizabethan Drama." *UTSE,* 21 (1942), 59–85.

743 RIBNER, Irving. "The Tudor History Play: An Essay in Definition." *PMLA,* 69 (1954), 591–609.

744 RIBNER, Irving. *The English History Play in the Age of Shakespeare.* Princeton: Princeton University Press, 1957. Rev. ed. London: Methuen, 1965.

745 SCHELLING, F. E. *The English Chronicle Play.* New York: Macmillan, 1902.

746 SMITH, Robert Metcalf. *Froissart and the English Chronicle Play.* New York: Columbia University Press, 1917.

747 TALBERT, Ernest W. *The Problem of Order.* Chapel Hill: University of North Carolina Press, 1962.

The Major Dramatists

Beaumont, Francis (1584–1616), and Fletcher, John (1579–1625)

Bibliography

748 PENNEL, Charles A., and W. P. WILLIAMS, eds. *Francis Beaumont, John Fletcher, Philip Massinger, 1937–1965; John Ford, 1940–1965; James Shirley, 1955–1965.* Elizabethan Bibliographies Supplements 8. London: Nether Press, 1968.

Works

749 *The Works of Francis Beaumont and John Fletcher.* 4 vols. A. H. Bullen, gen. ed. London: Bell, 1904–12.

750 *The Works of Francis Beaumont and John Fletcher.* 10 vols. Arnold Glover and A. R. Waller, eds. Cambridge: Cambridge University Press, 1905–12.

751 *The Dramatic Works in the Beaumont and Fletcher Canon.* Fredson T. Bowers, gen. ed. Cambridge: Cambridge University Press, 1966–.

752 *Songs and Lyrics from the Plays of Beaumont and Fletcher.* E. H. Fellowes, Ed. London: Etchells & Macdonald, 1928. [With Contemporary Musical Settings.]

753 *A King and No King.* Robert K. Turner, ed. Regents Renaissance Drama Series. Lincoln: University of Nebraska Press, 1963.

754 *The Knight of the Burning Pestle.* John Doebler, ed. Regents Renaissance Drama Series. Lincoln: University of Nebraska Press, 1967.

755 *The Knight of the Burning Pestle.* A. J. Gurr, ed. Fountainwell. Berkeley: University of California Press, 1968.

756 *The Knight of the Burning Pestle* Michael Hattaway, ed. New Mermaids. London: Bern, 1969.

757 *The Maid's Tragedy.* A. J. Gurr, ed. Fountainwell. Berkeley: University of California Press, 1969.

758 *The Maid's Tragedy.* H. B. Norland, ed. Regents Renaissance Drama Series. Lincoln: University of Nebraska Press, 1968.

759 *Philaster.* D. J. Ashe, ed. Regents Renaissance Drama Series. Lincoln: University of Nebraska Press, 1974.

760 *Philaster.* A. J. Gurr, ed. Revels Plays. Cambridge: Harvard University Press, 1969.

Studies

761 ABEND, Murray. "Shakespeare's Influences in Beaumont and Fletcher." *N&Q,* 197 (1952), 272–4, 360–3.

762 ADKINS, Mary G. M. "The Citizens in *Philaster:* Their Function and Significance." *SP,* 43 (1946), 203–12.

763 APPLETON, William W. *Beaumont and Fletcher, A Critical Study.* London: Allen & Unwin, 1956.

764 BALD, R. C. *Bibliographical Studies in the Beaumont and Fletcher Folio of 1647.* London: Oxford University Press, 1938.

765 BOND, R. Warwick. "On Six Plays in Beaumont and Fletcher, 1679." *RES,* 11 (1935), 257–75.

766 BROOKE, C. F. Tucker. "The Royal Fletcher and the Loyal Heywood." *Elizabethan Studies and Other Essays: In Honor of George F. Reynolds.* Boulder: University of Colorado Press, 1945. Pp. 192–94.

767 DANBY, John F. "Jacobean Absolutists: The Placing of Beaumont and Fletcher." *Cambridge Journal,* 3 (1950), 515–40.

768 DANBY, John F. *Poets on Fortune's Hill: Studies in Sidney, Shakespeare, Beaumont and Fletcher.* London: Faber, 1952.

769 DAVISON, Peter. "The Serious Concerns of *Philaster.*" *ELH,* 30 (1963), 1–15.

770 DOEBLER, John. "Beaumont's *Knight of the Burning Pestle* and the Prodigal Son Plays." *SEL,* 5 (1956), 333–44.

771 DOEBLER, John. "The Tone of the Jasper and Luce Scenes in Beaumont's *The Knight of the Burning Pestle.*" *ES,* 56 (1975), 108–13.

772 ECCLES, Mark. "Francis Beaumont's *Grammar Lecture.*" *RES,* 16 (1940), 402–14.

773 EDWARDS, Philip. "The Danger Not the Death: The Art of John Fletcher." *Jacobean Theatre.* Pp. 159–78. **276.**

774 FINKELPEARL, Philip J. "Beaumont, Fletcher, and 'Beaumont & Fletcher': Some Distinctions." *ELR,* 1 (1971), 144–64.

775 FORKER, Charles R. "*Wit Without Money: A Fletcherian Antecedent to Keep the Widow Waking.*" *CompD,* 8 (1974), 172–83.

776 GAYLEY, Charles M. *Francis Beaumont, Dramatist.* New York: Century, 1914.

777 GERRITSEN, Johan. "The Printing of the Beaumont and Fletcher Folio of 1647." *The Library,* 3 (1949), 233–64.

778 GOSSETT, Suzanne. "Masque Influence on the Dramaturgy of Beaumont and Fletcher." *MP,* 69 (1972), 199–208.

779 GOSSETT, Suzanne. "The Term 'Masque' in Shakespeare and Fletcher, and *The Coxcomb.*" *SEL,* 14 (1974), 285–96.

780 GRANT, R. Patricia. "Cervantes' *El casamiento engañoso* and Fletcher's *Rule a Wife and Have a Wife.*" *HR,* 12 (1944) 330–8.

781 GREG, W. W. "The Printing of the Beaumont and Fletcher Folio of 1647." *The Library,* n.s. 2 (1921), 109–15.

782 HARRISON, Thomas P., Jr. "A Probable Source of Beaumont and Fletcher's *Philaster.*" *PMLA,* 41 (1926), 294–303.

783 HOY, Cyrus. "The Shares of Fletcher and His Collaborators in the Beaumont and Fletcher Canon." *SB,* 8 (1956), 129–46; 9 (1957), 142–62; 11 (1958), 85–106; 12 (1959), 91–116; 13 (1960), 77–108; 14 (1961), 45–67; 15 (1962), 71–90.

784 INGRAM, R. W. "Patterns of Music and Action in Fletcherian Drama." *Music in English Renaissance Drama.* Pp. 75–95. **457.**

785 JEFFERY, Violet M. "Italian Influence in Fletcher's *Faithful Shepherdess.*" *MLR,* 21 (1926), 147–58.

786 LEECH, Clifford. *The John Fletcher Plays.* London: Chatto & Windus, 1962.

787 LINDSAY, Edwin S. "The Music of the Songs in Fletcher's Plays." *SP,* 21 (1924), 325–55.

788 LINDSAY, Edwin S. "The Original Music for Beaumont's Play *The Knight of the Burning Pestle.*" *SP,* 26 (1929), 425–43.

789 McKEITHAN, Daniel M. *The Debt to Shakespeare in Beaumont and Fletcher's Plays.* Austin: University of Texas Press, 1938.

790 MAKKINK, H. J. *Philip Massinger and John Fletcher: A Comparison.* Rotterdam: Nijgh & Van Ditman, 1927.

791 MAXWELL, Baldwin. "Fletcher and *Henry the Eighth.*" *Manly Anniversary Studies* (1923), 104–12. **See 219.**

792 MAXWELL, Baldwin. "The Hungry Knave in Beaumont and Fletcher's Plays." *PQ,* 5 (1926), 299–305.

793 MAXWELL, Baldwin. *Studies in Beaumont, Fletcher and Massinger.* Chapel Hill: University of North Carolina Press, 1939.

794 MINCOFF, Marco. "*The Faithful Shepherdess:* A Fletcherian Experiment." *RenD,* 9 (1966), 163–78.

795 MINCOFF, Marco. "Shakespeare, Fletcher and Baroque Tragedy." *SS,* 20 (1967), 1–15.

796 MIZENER, Arthur. "The High Design of *A King and No King.*" *MP,* 38 (1940–41), 133–54.

797 NEILL, Michael. " 'The Simetry, Which Gives a Poem Grace': Masque, Imagery, and the Fancy of *The Maid's Tragedy.*" *RenD,* n.s. 3 (1970), 111–36.

798 OLIPHANT, E. H. C. *The Plays of Beaumont and Fletcher; an Attempt to Determine Their Respective Shares and the Shares of Others.* New Haven: Yale University Press, 1927.

799 OLIPHANT, E. H. C. "The Plays of Beaumont and Fletcher: Some Additional Notes." *PQ,* 9 (1930), 7–22.

800 RULFS, Donald J. "Beaumont and Fletcher on the London Stage, 1776–1833." *PMLA,* 63 (1948), 1245–64.

801 SAVAGE, James E. "Beaumont and Fletcher's *Philaster* and Sidney's *Arcadia.*" *ELH,* 14 (1947), 194–206.

802 SAVAGE, James E. "The 'Gaping Wounds' in the Text of *Philaster.*" *PQ,* 28 (1949), 443–57.

803 SCHUTT, J. H. "*Philaster* Considered as a Work of Literary Art." *ES,* 6 (1924), 81–7.

804 SPRAGUE, Arthur Colby. *Beaumont and Fletcher on the Restoration Stage.* Cambridge: Harvard University Press, 1926.

805 STEIGER, Klaus, P. " 'May a Man be Caught with Faces?': The Convention of 'Heart' and 'Face' in Fletcher and Rowley's *The Maid in the Mill.*" *E&S 1966,* (1967), 47–63.

806 THORNDIKE, Ashley H. *The Influence of Beaumont and Fletcher on Shakespeare.* Worcester, Mass.: O. B. Wood, 1901.

807 TUPPER, James. "The Relation of the Heroic Play to the Romances of Beaumont and Fletcher." *PMLA*, 20 (1905), 584–621.

808 TURNER, Robert K., Jr. "The Morality of *A King and No King.*" *RenP 1959*, (1960), 93–103.

809 TURNER, Robert K., Jr. "The Relationship of *The Maid's Tragedy*, Q1 and Q2." *PBSA*, 51 (1957), 332–7.

810 UPTON, Albert W. "Allusions to James I and His Court in Marston's *Fawn* and Beaumont's *Woman Hater.*" *PMLA*, 44 (1929), 1048–65.

811 UPTON, Albert W. "The Authorship of *The Woman Hater.*" *PQ*, 9 (1930), 33–42.

812 WAITH, Eugene M. "Characterization in John Fletcher's Tragicomedies. *RES*, 19 (1943), 141–64.

813 WAITH, Eugene M. "John Fletcher and the Act of Declamation." *PMLA*, 66 (1951), 226–34.

814 WAITH, Eugene M. *The Pattern of Tragicomedy in Beaumont and Fletcher.* New Haven: Yale University Press, 1952.

815 WALLIS, Lawrence B. *Fletcher, Beaumont, and Company, Entertainers to the Jacobean Gentry.* New York: King's Crown Press, 1947.

816 WILSON, Harold S. "*Philaster* and *Cymbeline.*" English Institute Essays 1951. New York: Columbia University Press, 1952. Pp. 146–67.

817 WILSON, J. H. *The Influence of Beaumont and Fletcher on Restoration Drama.* Columbus: Ohio State University Press, 1928.

Brome, Richard (ca. 1590?–1652)

Works

818 *The Dramatic Works of Richard Brome Containing Fifteen Comedies.* 3 vols. London: John Pearson, 1873. Reprinted, New York: AMS Press, 1966.

819 *The Antipodes.* Ann Haaker, ed. Regents Renaissance Drama Series. Lincoln: University of Nebraska Press, 1966.

820 *A Jovial Crew.* Ann Haaker, ed. Regents Renaissance Drama Series. Lincoln: University of Nebraska Press, 1968.

Studies

821 ANDREWS, Clarence E. *Richard Brome: A Study of His Life and Works.* Yale Studies in English 46. New York: Holt, 1913.

822 COOK, Elizabeth. "The Plays of Richard Brome." *More Books*, 22 (1947), 285–301.

823 CROWTHER, John W. "The Literary History of Richard Brome's *A Joviall Crew.*" *Studies in English Renaissance Literature.* Waldo F. McNeir, ed. Baton Rouge: Louisiana State University Press, 1962. Pp. 132–48.

824 DAVIS, Joe Lee. "Richard Brome's Neglected Contribution to Comic Theory." *SP*, 40 (1943), 520–8.

825 DONALDSON, Ian. "Living Backward: *The Antipodes.*" *The World Upside-Down: Comedy from Jonson to Fielding.* Oxford: The Clarendon Press, 1970.

826 FAUST, E. K. R. *Richard Brome. Ein Beitrag zur Geschichte der englischen Litteratur.* Halle: H. John, 1887.

827 KAUFMANN, R. J. *Richard Brome, Caroline Playwright.* New York: Columbia University Press, 1961.

828 KAUFMANN, R. J. "Suckling and Davenant Satirized by Brome." *MLR,* 55 (1960), 332–44.

829 THALER, Alwin. "Was Richard Brome an Actor?" *MLN,* 36 (1921), 88–91.

Chapman, George (1559?–1634)

Bibliography

830 PENNEL, Charles A., and W. P. WILLIAMS, eds. *George Chapman, 1937–1965; John Marston, 1939–1965.* Elizabethan Bibliographies Supplements 4. London: Nether Press, 1968.

831 YAMADA, Akihiro. "George Chapman: A Checklist of Editions, Biography, and Criticism, 1946–1965." *RORD,* 10 (1967), 75–86.

832 RAY, George W. "George Chapman: A Checklist of Editions, Biography, and Criticism, 1946–1956—Addenda." *RORD,* 11 (1968), 55–8.

Works

833 *The Plays and Poems of George Chapman.* 2 vols. T. M. Parrott, ed. London: Routledge & Sons; *Comedies,* 1914, *Tragedies,* 1910. Reprinted, New York: Russell & Russell, 1961.

834 *The Plays of George Chapman: The Comedies.* Allan Holaday, gen. ed. Urbana: University of Illinois Press, 1970–.

835 *All Fools.* Frank Manley, ed. Regents Renaissance Drama Series. Lincoln: University of Nebraska Press, 1968.

836 *Bussy D'Ambois.* Nicholas Brooke, ed. Revels Plays. Cambridge: Harvard University Press, 1964.

837 *Bussy D'Ambois.* M. Evans, ed. New Mermaids. New York: Hill & Wang, 1966.

838 *Bussy D'Ambois.* R. J. Lordi, ed. Regents Renaissance Drama Series. Lincoln: University of Nebraska Press, 1964.

839 *The Gentleman Usher.* J. H. Smith, ed. Regents Renaissance Drama Series. Lincoln: University of Nebraska Press, 1970.

840 *The Widow's Tears.* E. M. Smeak. ed. Regents Renaissance Drama Series. Lincoln: University of Nebraska Press, 1966.

Studies

841 ADAMS, Robert P. "Critical Myths and Chapman's Original *Bussy D'Ambois.*" *RenD,* 9 (1966), 141–62.

842 AGGELER, Geoffrey. "The Unity of Chapman's *The Revenge of Bussy D'Ambois.*" *PCP,* 4 (1969), 5–18.

843 BARBER, C. L. "The Ambivalence of *Bussy D'Ambois.*" *REL,* 2 (1961), 38–44.

844 BATTENHOUSE, Roy W. "Chapman and the Nature of Man." *ELH,* 12 (1945), 87–107.

845 BEMENT, Peter. *George Chapman: Action and Contemplation in his Tragedies* Jacobean Drama Studies 8. Salzburg: Institut für Englische Sprache und Literatur, Universität Salzburg, 1974

846 BEMENT, Peter. "The Imagery of Darkness and of Light in Chapman's *Bussy D'Ambois.*" *SP,* 64 (1967), 187–98.

847 BEMENT, Peter. "The Stoicism of Chapman's Clermont D'Ambois." *SEL,* 12 (1972), 345–57.

848 BERGSON, Allen. "The Ironic Tragedies of Marston and Chapman: Notes on Jacobean Tragic Form." *JEGP,* 69 (1970, 613–30.

849 BRAUNMULLER, Albert R. "Chapman's Use of Plutarch's *De Fortuna Romanorum* in *The Tragedy of Charles, Duke of Byron.*" *RES,* 23 (1972), 178–9.

850 BRAUNMULLER, Albert R. " 'A Greater Wound': Corruption and Human Fraility in Chapman's *Chabot, Admiral of France.*" *MLR,* 70 (1975), 241–59.

851 BRODWIN, Leonora L. "Authorship of *The Second Maiden's Tragedy:* A Consideration of the MS Attribution to Chapman." *SP,* 63 (1966), 51–77.

852 BROUDE, Ronald. "George Chapman's Stoic-Christian Revenger." *SP,* 70 (1973), 51–61.

853 BROWN, John Russell. "Chapman's *Caesar and Pompey:* An Unperformed Play?" *MLR,* 49 (1954), 466–9.

854 BURBRIDGE, Roger T. "Speech and Action in Chapman's *Bussy D'Ambois.*" *TSL,* 17 (1972), 59–65.

855 BURTON, K. M. "The Political Tragedies of Chapman and Ben Jonson." *EIC,* 2 (1952), 397–412.

856 CRAIG, Hardin. "Ethics in the Jacobean Drama: The Case of Chapman." *Essays in Dramatic Literature.* Pp. 25–46. **See 279.**

857 CRAWLEY, Derek. *Character in Relation to Action in the Tragedies of George Chapman.* Jacobean Drama Studies 16. Salzburg: Institut für Englische Sprache und Literatur, Universität Salzburg, 1974.

858 CRAWLEY, Derek. "Decision and Character in Chapman's *The Tragedy of Caesar and Pompey.*" *SEL,* 7 (1966), 269–76.

859 CRAWLEY, Derek. "The Effect of Shirley's Hand on Chapman's *The Tragedy of Chabot Admiral of France.*" *SP,* 63 (1966), 677–96.

860 ECCLES, Mark. "Chapman's Early Years." *SP,* 43 (1946), 176–93.

861 ENGEL, Claire-Elaine. "Les Sources du *Bussy D'Ambois* de Chapman." *RLC,* 12, (1932), 587–95.

862 GABEL, John B. "The Original Version of Chapman's *Tragedy* of Byron." *JEGP,* 63 (1964), 433–40.

863 GOLDSTEIN, Leonard. *George Chapman: Aspects of Decadence in Early Seventeenth Century Drama.* 2 vols. Jacobean Drama Studies 31. Salzburg: Institut für Englische Sprache und Literatur, Universität Salzburg, 1975.

864 GRANT, Thomas M. *The Comedies of George Chapman: A Study in Development.* Jacobean Drama Studies 5. Salzburg: Institut für Englische Sprache und Literatur, Universität Salzburg, 1972.

865 HADDAKIN, Lilian. "Chapman's Use of Origen's 'Contra Celsum' in *The Tragedy of Caesar and Pompey.*" *N&Q,* 198 (1953), 147–48.

866 HADAKIN, Lillian. "A Note on Chapman and Two Medieval English Jurists." *MLR,* 47 (1952), 550–3.

867 HERRING, Thelma. "Chapman and an Aspect of Modern Criticism." *RenD,* 8 (1965), 153–79.

868 HIBBARD, G. R. "Goodness and Greatness: An Essay on the Tragedies of Ben Jonson and George Chapman." *RMS,* 11 (1968) 5–54.

869 HIGGINS, Michael H. "Chapman's 'Senecal Man.'" *RES,* 21 (1945), 183–91.

870 HIGGINS, Michael H. "The Development of the 'Senecal Man': Chapman's *Bussy D'Ambois* and Some Precursors." *RES,* 23 (1947), 24–33.

871 HIGGINS, Michael H. "George Chapman: Tragedy and the Providential View of History." *SS,* 20 (1967), 27–31.

872 HOGAN, A. P. "Thematic Unity in Chapman's *Monsieur D'Olive.*" *SEL,* 11 (1971), 295–306.

873 HOMAN, Sidney, R., Jr. "Chapman and Marlowe: The Paradoxical Hero and the Divided Response." *JEGP,* 68 (1969), 391–406.

874 INGLEDEW, J. E. "Chapman's Use of Lucan in *Caesar and Pompey.*" *RES,* 13 (1962), 283–88.

875 JACQUOT, Jean. "*Bussy D'Ambois* and Chapman's Conception of Tragedy." *English Studies Today.* G. A. Bonnard, ed. Bern: Franke Verlag, 1961. Pp. 129–41.

876 JACQUOT, Jean. *George Chapman, sa vie, sa poésie, son théâtre, sa pensée.* Paris: Les Belles Lettres, 1951.

877 JONES, Marion, and Glynne WICKHAM. "The Stage Furnishings of George Chapman's *The Tragedy of Charles Duke of Biron.*" *TN,* 16 (1962), 113–17.

878 KAUFMAN, Helen "*The Blind Beggar of Alexandria:* A Reappraisal." *PQ,* 38 (1959), 101–6.

879 KENNEDY, Charles W. "Political Theory in the Plays of George Chapman." *Essays in Dramatic Literature.* Pp. 73–86. See **279.**

880 KREIDER, Paul V. *Elizabethan Comic Character Conventions as Revealed in the Comedies of George Chapman.* Ann Arbor: University of Michigan Press, 1935.

881 MacCOLLOM, William G. "The Tragic Hero and Chapman's *Bussy D'Ambois.*" *UTQ,* 18 (1949), 227–33.

882 MacLURE, Millar. *George Chapman: A Critical Study.* Toronto: University of Toronto Press, 1966.

883 MUIR, Edwin. "'Royal Man': Notes on the Tragedies of George Chapman." *Essays on Literature and Society.* London: The Hogarth Press, 1949. Pp. 20–30.

884 NICOLL, Allardyce. "The Dramatic Portrait of George Chapman." *PQ,* 41 (1962), 215–28.

885 ORANGE, Linwood E. "*Bussy D'Ambois:* The Web of Pretense." *SoQ,* 8 (1969), 37–56.

886 ORNSTEIN, Robert. "The Dates of Chapman's Tragedies Once More." *MP,* 69 (1961), 61–4.

887 PAGNINI, Marcello. *Forme e Motivi nella Poesie e nelle Tragedie di George Chapman.* Firenze: Valmartina, 1958.

888 PERKINSON, Richard H. "Nature and the Tragic Hero in Chapman's Bussy Plays." *MLQ,* 3 (1942), 263–85.

889 POGRELL, N., von. *Die philosophisch-poetische Entwicklung George Chapmans: Ein Versuch zur Interpretation seines Werkes.* Hamburg: Friederichsen, 1939.

890 PRESSON, Robert K. "Wrestling with This World: A View of George Chapman." *PMLA,* 84 (1969), 44–50.

891 REES, Ennis. "Chapman's *Blind Beggar* and the Marlovian Hero." *JEGP,* 57 (1958), 60–3.

892 REES, Ennis. *The Tragedies of George Chapman: Renaissance Ethics in Action.* Cambridge: Harvard University Press, 1954.

893 REESE, Jack E. "Potiphar's Wife' and Other Folk Tales in Chapman's *Blind Beggar of Alexandria.*" *TSL,* 18 (1973), 33–48.

894 RIBNER, Irving. "Character and Theme in Chapman's *Bussy D'Ambois.*" *ELH,* 26 (1959), 482–96.

895 RIBNER, Irving. "The Meaning of Chapman's *Tragedy of Chabot.*" *MLR,* 55 (1960), 321–31.

896 ROBERTSON, Jean. "The Early Life of George Chapman." *MLR,* 40 (1945), 157–65.

897 SCHOENBAUM, S. "The 'Deformed Mistress' Theme and Chapman's *Gentleman Usher.*" *N&Q,* n.s. 7 (1960), 22–4.

898 SCHOENBAUM, S. "*The Widow's Tears* and the Other Chapman." *HLQ,* 23 (1960), 321–38.

899 SCHWARTZ, Elias. "Chapman's Renaissance Man: Byron Reconsidered." *JEGP,* 58 (1959), 613–26.

900 SCHWARTZ, Elias. "The Date of *Bussy D'Ambois.*" *MP,* 59 (1961), 126–7.

901 SCHWARTZ, Elias. "The Date of Chapman's Byron Plays." *MP,* 58 (1961), 201–2.

902 SCHWARTZ, Elias. "The Dates and Order of Chapman's Tragedies." *MP,* 57 (1959), 80–2.

903 SCHWARTZ, Elias. "A Neglected Play by Chapman [*Caesar and Pompey*]," *SP,* 58 (1961), 140–59.

904 SCHWARTZ, Elias. "Seneca, Homer, and Chapman's *Bussy D'Ambois.*" *JEGP,* 56 (1957), 163–76.

905 SISSON, C. J. and R. BUTMAN. "George Chapman, 1612–22, Some New Facts." *MLR,* 46 (1951), 185–90.

906 SMITH, James. "George Chapman." *Scrutiny,* 13 (1935), 339–50.

907 SOLVE, Norma Dobie. *Stuart Politics in Chapman's "Tragedy of Chabot."* Ann Arbor: University of Michigan Press, 1929.

908 SPENS, Janet. "Chapman's Ethical Thought." *E&S,* 11 (1925), 145–69.

909 SPIVACK, Charlotte. *George Chapman.* New York: Twayne, 1967.

910 STAGG, Louis C. *An Index to the Figurative Language of George Chapman's Tragedies.* Charlottesville: Bibliographical Society of the University of Virginia, 1970.

911 STURMAN, Berta. "The 1641 Edition of Chapman's *Bussy D'Ambois.*" *HLQ,* 14 (1951), 171–201.

912 TRICOMI, Albert H. "The Revised *Bussy D'Ambois* and *The Revenge of Bussy D'Ambois:* Joint Performance in Thematic Counterpoint." *ELN,* 9 (1972), 253–62.

913 TRICOMI, Albert H. "The Social Disorder of Chapman's *The Widow's Tears.*" *JEGP,* 72 (1973), 350–9.

914 URE, Peter. "Chapman as Translator and Tragic Playwright." *The Age of Shakespeare.* Pelican Guide to English Literature 2. Baltimore: Penguin, 1955. Pp. 318–33.

915 URE, Peter. "Chapman's Tragedies." *Jacobean Theatre.* Pp. 227–48. **See 276.**

916 URE, Peter. "Chapman's *Tragedy of Bussy D'Ambois:* Problems of the Revised Quarto." *MLR,* 48 (1953), 257–69.

917 URE, Peter. "Chapman's *Tragedy of Byron.*" *MLR,* 54 (1959), 557–8.

918 URE, Peter. "Chapman's Use of North's Plutarch in *Caesar and Pompey.*" *RES,* 9 (1958), 281–4.

919 URE, Peter. "The Main Outline of Chapman's *Byron.*" *SP,* 47 (1950), 568–88.

920 WADDINGTON, Raymond B. "Prometheus and Hercules: The Dialectic of *Bussy D'Ambois.*" *ELH,* 34 (1967), 21–48.

921 WEIDNER, Henry M. "The Dramatic Uses of Homeric Idealism: The Significance of Theme and Design in George Chapman's *The Gentleman Usher.*" *ELH,* 28 (1961), 121–36.

922 WEIDNER, Henry M. "Homer and the Fallen World: Focus of Satire in George Chapman's *The Widows' Tears.*" *JEGP,* 62 (1963), 518–32.

923 WIELER, John W. *George Chapman—The Effect of Stoicism Upon His Tragedies.* New York: King's Crown Press, 1949.

924 WILKES, G. A. "Chapman's 'Lost' Play, *The Fount of New Fashions.*" *JEGP,* 62 (1963), 77–81.

925 WILLIAMSON, Marilyn L. "Matter of More Mirth." *RenP 1956,* (1957), 34–41.

Dekker, Thomas (1570?–1641?)

Bibliography

926 DONOVAN, Dennis, ed. *Thomas Dekker, 1945–1965; Thomas Heywood, 1938–1965; Cyril Tourneur, 1945–1965.* Elizabethan Bibliographies Supplement 2. London: Nether Press, 1967.

Works

927 *The Dramatic Works of Thomas Dekker.* 4 vols. Fredson T. Bowers, ed. Cambridge: Cambridge University Press, 1953–61.

928 *Lust's Dominion.* J. LeGay Brereton, ed. Louvain: Uystpruyst, 1931.

929 *The Shoemaker's Holiday.* David J. Palmer, ed. New Mermaids. London: Benn, 1975.

930 *The Shoemaker's Holiday.* P. Davies, ed. Fountainwell. Berkeley: University of California Press, 1968.

Studies

931 ADKINS, Mary G. M. "Puritanism in the Plays of and Pamphlets of Thomas Dekker." *UTSE,* 18 (1939), 86–113.

932 ASHTON, J. W. "Dekker's Use of Folklore in *Old Fortunatus, If This Be Not a Good Play,* and *The Witch of Edmonton.*" *PQ,* 41 (1962), 240–8.

933 BAIRD, Matthew. "The Early Editions of Thomas Dekker's *The Converted Courtesan* or *The Honest Whore, Part I.*" *The Library,* n.s. 10 (1929), 52–60.

934 BENBOW, R. Mark. "Thomas Dekker and Some Cures for the 'City Gout.'" *YES,* 5 (1975), 52–69.

935 BERGERON, David M. "Thomas Dekker's Lord Mayor's Shows." *ES,* 51 (1970), 2–15.

936 BERLIN, Normand. "Thomas Dekker: A Partial Reappraisal." *SEL,* 6 (1966), 263–78.

937 BLOW, Suzanne. *Rhetoric in the Plays of Thomas Dekker.* Jacobean Drama Studies 3. Salzburg: Institut für Englische Sprache und Literatur, Universität Salzburg, 1972.

938 BOWERS, Fredson T. "Bibliographical Problems in Dekker's Magnificent Entertainment." *The Library,* n.s. 17 (1937), 333–9.

939 BOWERS, Fredson T. "Essex's Rebellion and Dekker's *Old Fortunatus.*" *RES,* 3 (1952), 365–6.

940 BRADFORD, Gamaliel. "The Women of Dekker." *SR,* 33 (1925), 284–90.

941 BROWN, Arthur. "Citizen Comedy and Domestic Drama." *Jacobean Theatre.* Pp. 63–84. **See 276.**

942 BURELBACH, Frederick. "War and Peace in *The Shoemaker's Holiday.*" *TSL,* 13 (1968), 99–107.

943 CHAMPION, Larry S. "From Melodrama to Comedy: A Study of the Dramatic Perspective in Dekker's *The Honest Whore, Parts I and II.*" *SP,* 69 (1972), 192–209.

944 CHANDLER, W. K. "Sources of Characters in *The Shoemaker's Holiday.*" *MP,* 27 (1929), 175–82.

945 CHANDLER, W. K. "Topography of *The Shoemaker's Holiday.*" *SP,* 26 (1929), 499–505.

946 CONOVER, James. *Thomas Dekker: An Analysis of Dramatic Structure.* The Hague: Mouton, 1969.

947 GREGG, K. L. *Thomas Dekker: A Study in Economic and Social Backgrounds.* Seattle: University of Washington Press, 1924.

948 HOWARTH, R. G. "Dekker Not a Merchant Taylor." *N&Q,* 199 (1954), 52.

949 HUNT, Mary L. *Thomas Dekker.* New York: Columbia University Press, 1911.

950 JONES-DAVIES, M. T. *Un Peintre de la Vie Londoniènne: Thomas Dekker.* 2 vols. Paris: Didier, 1958.

951 JONES-DAVIES, M. T. "Source du Latin scolastique dans *The Whore of Babylon* de Thomas Dekker." *EA,* 6 (1953), 142–3.

952 JONES-DAVIES, M. T. "Thomas Dekker et les Marchands-Tailleurs." *EA,* 6 (1953), 50–3.

953 KAPLAN, Joel H. "Virtue's Holiday: Thomas Dekker and Simon Eyre." *RenD,* n.s. 2 (1969), 103–22.

954 KINNEY, Arthur F. "Thomas Dekker's *Twelfth Night.*" *UTQ,* 41 (1971), 63–73.

955 KISTNER, A. L. and M. K. KISTNER. "*I Honest Whore:* A Comedy of Blood." *HAB,* 23, iv(1972), 23–7.

956 LAW, Robert Adger. "*The Shoemaker's Holiday* and *Romeo and Juliet.*" *SP,* 21 (1924), 356–61.

957 MANHEIM, L. M. "The King in Dekker's *The Shoemaker's Holiday.*" *N&Q,* n.s. 4 (1957), 432–3.

958 MANHEIM, Michael. "The Construction of *The Shoemaker's Holiday.*" *SEL,* 10 (1970), 315–23.

959 MANHEIM, Michael. "The Thematic Structure of Dekker's *Honest Whore.*" *SEL,* 5 (1956), 363–81.

960 MAUGERI, Aldo. *Studi su Thomas Dekker.* Messina: Grafiche la Sicilia, 1958.

961 MURRAY, Peter B. "The Collaboration of Dekker and Webster in *Northward Ho* and *Westward Ho.*" *PBSA,* 56 (1962), 482–6.

962 NOVARR, David. "Dekker's Gentle Craft and the Lord Mayor of London." *MP,* 57 (1960), 233–9.

963 PRICE, George R. *Thomas Dekker.* New York: Twayne, 1968.

964 ROBBINS, Larry M. *Thomas Dekker's* "A Knights Conjuring" (1607): *A Critical Edition.* Studies in English Literature 78. The Hague: Mouton, 1974.

965 SACKVILLE-WEST, Edward. "The Significance of *The Witch of Edmonton.*" *Criterion,* 17 (1937), 23–32.

966 SHIRLEY, Peggy Faye. *Serious and Tragic Elements in the Comedy of Thomas Dekker.* Jacobean Drama Studies 50. Salzburg: Institut für Englische Sprache und Literatur, Universität Salzburg, 1975.

967 SIMMONS, J. L. "*Lust's Dominion:* A Showpiece for the Globe." *Tulane Studies in English,* 20 (1972), 11–22.

968 SPENDER, Constance. "The Plays of Thomas Dekker." *Contemporary Review,* 130 (1926), 332–9.

969 SYKES, H. Dugdale. "Massinger and Dekker's *The Virgin Martyr.*" *N&Q,* 12th series 10 (1922), 61–5, 83–8.

970 THIEME, Heinz. *Zur Verfasserfrage des Dekkerschen Stückes "The Pleasant Comedy of Old Fortunatus."* Dresden: Risse, 1934.

971 THOMSON, Patricia. "The Old Way and the New Way in Dekker and Massinger." *MLR,* 51 (1956), 168–78.

972 TOLIVER, Harold E. "*The Shoemaker's Holiday:* Theme and Image." *BUSE,* 5 (1961), 208–18.

973 URE, Peter. "Patient Madman and Honest Whore: The Middleton-Dekker Oxymoron." *E&S 1966,* 18–40.

Ford, John (1586–1639?)

Bibliography

974 PENNEL, and WILLIAMS, eds. See **748.**

Works

975 *The Dramatic Works of John Ford.* 2 vols. William Gifford, ed. London: John Murray, 1827.

976 *John Ford's Dramatic Works.* 2 vols. W. Bang and Henry De Vocht, eds. Louvain: Uystpruyst; vol. 1, 1908, vol. 2, 1927.

977 *The Broken Heart.* D. K. Anderson, ed. Regents Renaissance Drama Series. Lincoln: University of Nebraska Press, 1968.

978 *The Broken Heart.* B. Morris, ed. New Mermaids. New York: Hill & Wang, 1966.

979 *The Chronicle History of Perkin Warbeck: A Strange Truth.* Peter Ure, ed. Revels Plays. Cambridge: Harvard University Press, 1968.

980 *Perkin Warbeck.* D. K. Anderson, ed. Regents Renaissance Drama Series. Lincoln: University of Nebraska Press, 1965.

981 *'Tis Pity She's a Whore.* N. W. Bawcutt, ed. Regents Renaissance Drama Series. Lincoln: University of Nebraska Press, 1966.

982 *'Tis Pity She's a Whore.* B. Morris, ed. New Mermaids. New York: Hill & Wang, 1969.

983 *'Tis Pity She's a Whore.* Derek Roper, ed. Revels Plays. London: Methuen; New York: Barnes & Noble, 1975.

Studies

984 ALI, Florence. *Opposing Absolutes: Conviction and Convention in John Ford's Plays.* Jacobean Drama Studies 44. Salzburg: Institut für Englische Sprache und Literatur, Universität Salzburg, 1974.

985 ANDERSON, D. K. "The Heart and the Banquet: Imagery in Ford's *'Tis Pity* and *The Broken Heart.*" *SEL,* 2 (1962), 209–17.

986 ANDERSON, D. K. *John Ford.* New York: Twayne, 1972.

987 ANDERSON, D. K. "Kingship in Ford's *Perkin Warbeck.*" *ELH,* 27 (1960), 177–93.

988 ANDERSON, D. K. "*Richard II* and *Perkin Warbeck.*" *SQ,* 13 (1962), 260–3.

989 BABB, Lawrence. "Abnormal Psychology in John Ford's *Perkin Warbeck.*" *MLN,* 51 (1936), 234–7.

990 BACON, Wallace. "The Literary Reputation of John Ford." *HLQ,* 11 (1947–78), 181–99.

991 BARISH, Jonas. *"Perkin Warbeck* as Anti-History." *EIC,* 20 (1970), 151–71.

992 BLAYNEY, Glenn H. "Convention, Plot, and Structure in *The Broken Heart.*" *MP,* 56 (1958), 1–9.

993 BOSE, Tirthankar. "Ford's Understanding of Honour." *LCrit,* 8 (1969), 19–26.

994 BRISSENDEN, Alan. "Impediments to Love: A Theme in John Ford." *RenD,* 7 (1964), 95–102.

995 BURBRIDGE, Roger T. "The Moral Vision in Ford's *The Broken Heart.*" *SEL,* 10 (1970), 397–407.

996 CARSANGIA, Giovanni M. " 'The Truth' in John Ford's *The Broken Heart.*" *CL,* 10 (1958), 344–8.

997 CHAMPION, Larry S. "Ford's *'Tis Pity She's a Whore* and the Jacobean Tragic Perspective." *PMLA,* 90 (1975), 78–87.

998 COCHNOWER, Mary Edith. "John Ford." *Seventeenth Century Studies.* Robert Shafer, ed. Princeton: Princeton University Press, 1933. Pp. 123–75.

999 DAVRIL, Robert. *Le Drame de John Ford.* Paris: Bibliothèque des Langues Modernes, 1954.

1000 DAVRIL, Robert. "John Ford et les Caractères overburiens." *EA,* 6 (1953), 122–6.

1001 DAVRIL, Robert. "Shakespeare and Ford." *ShJ,* 94 (1958) 121–31.

1002 EWING, S. B., Jr. *Burtonian Melancholy in the Plays of John Ford.* Princeton: Princeton University Press, 1940.

1003 GREENFIELD, Thelma N. "The Language of Process in Ford's *The Broken Heart.*" *PMLA,* 87 (1972), 397–405.

1004 HARBAGE, Alfred B. "The Mystery of *Perkin Warbeck.*" *Studies in the English Renaissance Drama.* Pp. 125–41. **See 270.**

1005 HOMAN, Sidney R. "Shakespeare and Dekker as Keys to Ford's *'Tis Pity She's a Whore.*" *SEL,* 7 (1967), 269–76.

1006 HOY, Cyrus. " 'Ignorance in Knowledge': Marlowe's Faustus and Ford's Giovanni." *MP,* 57 (1960), 145–54.

1007 KAUFMANN, R. J. "Ford's Tragic Perspective." *TSLL,* 1 (1960), 522–37.

1008 KAUFMANN, R. J. "Ford's 'Waste Land': *The Broken Heart.*" *RenD,* n.s. 3 (1970), 167–88.

1009 KELLY, Michael J. "The Values of Action and Chronicle in *The Broken Heart.*" *PLL,* 7 (1971), 150–8.

1010 KISTNER, Arthur L. and M. K. KISTNER. "The Dramatic Functions of Love in the Tragedies of John Ford." *SP,* 70 (1973), 62–76.

1011 KISTNER, Arthur L. and M. K. KISTNER. "The Fine Balance of Imposture in John Ford's *Perkin Warbeck.*" *ES,* 52 (1971), 419–23.

1012 LAUREN, Barbara. "John Ford: A Caroline Alternative to Beaumont and Fletcher." *MLS,* 5,i(1975), 53–66.

1013 LEECH, Clifford. *John Ford and the Drama of His Time.* London: Chatto & Windus, 1957.

1014 McDONALD, Charles O. "The Design of John Ford's *The Broken Heart:* A Study in the Development of Caroline Sensibility." *SP,* 59 (1962), 141–61.

1015 McMASTER, Juliet. "John Ford, Dramatist of Frustration." *English Studies in Canada*, 1 (1975), 266–79.

1016 McMASTER, Juliet. "Love, Lust and Sham: Structural Pattern in the Plays of John Ford." *RenD*, n.s. 2 (1969), 157–66.

1017 MALOUF, David. "The Dramatist as Critic: John Ford and *The Broken Heart*." *SoRA*, 5 (1972), 197–206.

1018 O'CONNOR, John J. "A Lost Play of Perkin Warbeck." *MLN*, 70 (1955), 566–8.

1019 O'CONNOR, John J. "William Warner and Ford's *Perkin Warbeck*." *N&Q*, 200 (1955), 233–5.

1020 OLIVER, H. J. *The Problem of John Ford*. Melbourne: Melbourne University Press, 1955.

1021 ORBISON, Tucker. *The Tragic Vision of John Ford*. Jacobean Drama Studies 21. Salzburg: Institut für Englische Sprache und Literatur, Universität Salzburg, 1974.

1022 PELLIZZI, Giovanna. "The Speech of Ithocles on Ambition and Ford's *The Broken Heart*." *English Miscellany*, 20 (1969), 93–100.

1023 PRAZ, Mario. *Il Dramma elisabettiano: Webster—Ford*. Rome: Ed. "Studium Orbis," 1946.

1024 REQUA, Kenneth A. "Music in the Ear: Giovanni as Tragic Hero in Ford's *'Tis Pity She's a Whore*." *PLL*, 7 (1971), 13–25.

1025 ROBERTS, Jeanne A. "John Ford's Passionate Abstractions." *SHR*, 7 (1973), 322–32.

1026 ROSEN, Carol C. "The Language of Cruelty in Ford's *'Tis Pity She's a Whore*." *CompD*, 8 (1974), 356–68.

1026A SARGEAUNT, M. Joan. *John Ford*. Oxford: Basil Blackwell, 1935.

1027 SARGEAUNT, M. Joan. "John Ford at the Middle Temple." *RES*, 8 (1932), 69–71.

1028 SENSABAUGH, G. F. "Another Play by John Ford." *MLQ*, 3 (1942), 595–601.

1029 SENSABAUGH, G. F. "Burton's Influence on Ford's *The Lover's Melancholy*." *SP*, 33 (1936), 545–71.

1030 SENSABAUGH, G. F. "Ford's Tragedy of Love-Melancholy." *ES*, 73 (1939), 212–9.

1031 SENSABAUGH, G. F. "John Ford and Elizabethan Tragedy." *Renaissance Studies in Honor of Hardin Craig*. Stanford: Stanford University Press, 1941. Pp. 250–61. [Also in *PQ*, 20 (1941), 442–53.]

1032 SENSABAUGH, G. F. "John Ford and Platonic Love in Court." *SP*, 36 (1939), 206–26.

1033 SENSABAUGH, G. F. "John Ford Revisited." *SEL*, 4 (1964), 195–216.

1034 SENSABAUGH, G. F. *The Tragic Muse of John Ford*. Palo Alto, Calif.: Stanford University Press, 1944.

1035 STAVIG, Mark. *John Ford and the Traditional Moral Order*. Madison: University of Wisconsin Press, 1968.

1036 STRUBLE, Mildred G. "The Indebtedness of Ford's *Perkin Warbeck* to Gainsford." *Anglia*, 49 (1925), 80–91.

1037 SUTTON, Juliet. "Ford's Use of Burton's Imagery." *N&Q,* 208 (1963), 415.

1038 SUTTON, Juliet. "Platonic Love in Ford's *The Fancies, Chaste and Noble." SEL,* 7 (1967), 299–309.

1039 SYKES, H. Dugdale. "John Ford, the Author of *The Spanish Gipsy." MLR,* 19 (1924), 11–24.

1040 URE, Peter. "Cult and Initiates in Ford's *Love's Sacrifice." MLQ,* 11 (1950), 298–306.

1041 URE, Peter. "Marriage and the Domestic Drama in Heywood and Ford." *ES,* 32 (1951), 200–16.

1042 WEATHERS, Winston. "*Perkin Warbeck:* A Seventeenth-Century Psychological Play." *SEL,* 4 (1964), 217–26.

Gascoigne, George (1525?–1577)

Bibliography

1043 JOHNSON, Robert C., ed. *Minor Elizabethans: Roger Ascham, 1946–1966; George Gascoigne, 1941–1966; John Heywood, 1944–1966; Thomas Kyd, 1940–1966; Anthony Munday, 1941–1966.* Elizabethan Bibliographies Supplements 9. London: Nether Press, 1968.

Works

1044 *The Complete Poems of George Gascoigne.* W. Carew Hazlitt, ed. London: The Roxburghe Library, 1869–70.

1045 *The Complete Works of George Gascoigne.* 2 vols. John W. Cunliffe, ed. Cambridge: Cambridge University Press, 1907–10.

Studies

1046 DUCLOS, Paul-Charles. "George Gascoigne, Ecuyer. Poète, prosateur, dramaturge et polyglotte anglais de la Renaissance." *RLV,* 19 (1953), 40–8.

1047 JOHNSON, Ronald C. *George Gascoigne.* New York: Twayne, 1972.

1048 PROUTY, C. T. *George Gascoigne, Elizabethan Courtier, Soldier and Poet.* New York: Columbia University Press, 1942.

1049 SCHELLING, F. E. *The Life and Writings of George Gascoigne.* Philadelphia: University of Pennsylvania Press, 1893.

Greene, Robert (ca. 1560–1592)

Bibliography

1050 Dean, J. S., Jr., ed. "Robert Greene; An addendum and Supplementary Bibliography of Editions, Biography, and Criticism, 1945–69." *RORD,* 13–14 (1972), 181–6.

1051 HAYASHI, Tetsumaro, ed. *Robert Greene Criticism: A Comprehensive Bibliography.* Metuchen, N.J.: Scarecrow, 1971.

1052 JOHNSON, Robert C., ed. *Robert Greene, 1945–1965; Thomas Lodge, 1939–1965; John Lyly, 1939–1965; Thomas Nashe, 1941–1965; George Peele, 1939–1965.* Elizabethan Bibliographies Supplements 5. London: Nether Press, 1968.

Works

1053 *The Life and Complete Works in Prose and Verse of Robert Greene.* 15 vols. A. B. Grosart, ed. London: The Huth Library, 1881–86. Reissued, New York: Russell & Russell, 1964.

1054 *The Plays and Poems of Robert Greene.* 2 vols. John Churton Collins, ed. Oxford: The Clarendon Press, 1905.

1055 *Friar Bacon and Friar Bungay.* Daniel Seltzer, ed. Regents Renaissance Drama Series. Lincoln: University of Nebraska Press, 1963.

1056 *Friar Bacon and Friar Bungay.* J. A. Lavin, ed. New Mermaid. New York: Hill & Wang, 1969.

1057 *James IV.* J. A. Lavin, ed. New Mermaid. New York: Hill & Wang, 1967.

1058 *JAMES IV.* Norman Sanders, ed. The Revels Plays. London: Methuen, 1970.

Studies

1059 ASSARSSON-RIZZI, Kerstin. *"Friar Bacon and Friar Bungay": A Structural and Thematic Analysis of Robert Greene's Play.* Lund: Gleerup, 1972.

1060 BABULA, William. "Fortune or Fate: Ambiguity in Robert Greene's *Orlando Furioso."* MLR, 67 (1972), 481–5.

1061 BRAUNMULLER, Albert R. "The Serious Comedy of Greene's *James IV."* *ELR,* 3 (1973), 335–50.

1062 DEAN, J. S., Jr. "Robert Greene's Romantic Heroines: Caught up in Knowledge and Power?" *BSUF,* 14 (1973), 3–12.

1063 ELLIS-FERMOR, Una M. "Marlowe and Greene: A Note on Their Relations as Dramatic Artists." *Studies in Honor of T. W. Baldwin.* Pp. 136–49. **See 269.**

1064 GELBER, Norman. "Robert Greene's *Orlando Furioso:* A Study in Thematic Ambiguity." *MLR,* 64 (1969), 264–6.

1065 HAYASHI, Tetsumaro. *"Orlando Furioso,* Robert Greene's Romantic Comedy." *Studia Anglica Posnaniensia,* 6 i–ii(1975), 157–60.

1066 HUDSON, Ruth. "Greene's *James IV* and Contemporary Allusions." *PMLA,* 47 (1932), 652–67.

1067 JACQUOT, Jean. "Ralegh's 'Hellish Verses' and the *Tragicall Raigne of Selimus.*" *MLR,* 48 (1953), 1–9.

1068 JORDAN, J. C. *Robert Greene.* New York: Columbia University Press, 1915. Reprinted, New York: Octagon, 1965.

1069 LAW, Robert Adger. "*A Looking Glass* and the Scriptures." *UTSE,* 19 (1940), 31–47.

1070 LIEVSAY, John L. "Robert Greene, Master of Arts, and 'Mayster Guazzo." *SP,* 36 (1939), 577–96.

1071 MACLAINE, A. H. "Greene's Borrowings from his Own Prose Fiction in *Friar Bacon and Friar Bungay* and *James the Fourth.*" *PQ,* 30 (1951), 22–9.

1072 McNEAL, Thomas H. "The Literary Origins of Robert Greene." *Shakespeare Association Bulletin,* 14 (1939), 176–81.

1073 McNEIR, Waldo. "The Original of Ateukin in Greene's *James IV.*" *MLN,* 62 (1947), 376–81.

1074 McNEIR, Waldo. "Robert Greene and *John of Bordeaux.*" *PMLA,* 64 (1949), 781–801.

1075 McNEIR, Waldo. "Traditional Elements in the Character of Greene's Friar Bacon." *SP,* 45 (1948), 172–9.

1076 MASON, E. C. "Satire on Women and Sex Tragedy." *ES,* 31 (1950), 1–10.

1077 MORTENSON, Peter. "*Friar Bacon and Friar Bungay:* Festive Comedy and 'Three-Form'd Luna.'" *ELR,* 2 (1972), 194–207.

1078 MUIR, Kenneth. "Robert Greene as Dramatist." *Essays on Shakespeare and Elizabethan Drama.* Pp. 45–54. See **287.**

1079 NELSON, Malcolm A. "The Sources of *George a Greene, The Pinner of Wakefield.*" *PQ,* 42 (1963), 159–65.

1080 PARR, Johnstone. "Robert Greene and his Classmates at Cambridge." *PMLA,* 77 (1962), 536–43.

1081 PRICE, Hereward T. "Shakespeare and His Young Contemporaries." *PQ,* 41 (1962), 37–57.

1082 RIBNER, Irving. "Greene's Attack on Marlowe: Some Light on *Alphonsus* and *Selimus.*" *SP,* 52 (1955), 162–71.

1083 ROUND, Percy Z. "Greene's Materials for *Friar Bacon and Friar Bungay.*" *MLN,* 21 (1926), 19–23.

1084 RUSSELL, Patricia. "Romantic Narrative Plays, 1570–1590." *Early Shakespeare.* Pp. 107–29. See **275.**

1085 SANDERS, Norman. "The Comedy of Greene and Shakespeare." *Early Shakespeare.* Pp. 35–53. See **275.**

1086 SAUNDERS, Chauncey E. "Robert Greene and His 'Editors.'" *PMLA,* 48 (1935), 392–417.

1087 SENN, Werner. *Studies in the Dramatic Construction of Robert Greene and George Peele.* Bern: Francke, 1973.

1088 STOROJENKO, N. *Robert Greene: His Life and Works.* See **1053.** Vol. 1, *passim.*

1089 SYKES, H. Dugdale. "Robert Greene and *George a Greene, the Pinner of Wakefield.*" *RES,* 7 (1931), 129–36.

1090 TOWNE, Frank. " 'White Magic' in *Friar Bacon and Friar Bungay*." *MLN*, 67 (1952), 9–13.

1091 WERTHEIM, Albert. "The Presentation of Sin in *Friar Bacon and Friar Bungay*." *Criticism*, 16 (1974), 273–86.

1092 WEST, Robert H. "White Magic in *Friar Bacon*." *MLN*, 67 (1952), 499–500.

Heywood, John (ca. 1497–1578)

Bibliography

1093 JOHNSON, ed. See **1043.**

Works

1094 *The Dramatic Writings of John Heywood.* John S. Farmer, ed. London: Early English Drama Society, 1905.

1095 *John Heywood's Works and Miscellaneous Short Poems.* Burton A. Milligan, ed. Urbana: University of Illinois Press, 1956.

Studies

1096 BEVINGTON, David M. "Is John Heywood's *Play of the Weather* Really About the Weather?" *RenD*, 7 (1964), 11–9.

1097 BOLWELL, Robert W. *The Life and Works of John Heywood.* New York: Columbia University Press, 1921.

1098 CAMERON, K. W. *Authorship and Sources of "Gentleness and Nobility": A Study in Early Tudor Drama.* Raleigh, N.C.: Thistle Press, 1941. [Together with a text of the play based on the black-letter original.]

1099 CAMERON, K. W. *The Background of John Heywood's "Witty and Witless": A Study in Early Tudor Drama.* Raleigh, N.C.: Thistle Press, 1941.

1100 CAMERON, K. W. *John Heywood's "Play of the Weather": A Study in Early Tudor Drama.* Raleigh, N.C.: Thistle Press, 1941.

1101 CAMERON, K. W. "The True Source of John Heywood's *Johan Johan.*" *MLR*, 45 (1950), 289–95.

1102 CRAIK, T. W. "Experiment and Variety in John Heywood's Plays." *RenD*, 7 (1964), 6–11.

1103 DE LA BÈRE, R. *John Heywood: Entertainer.* London: Allen & Unwin, 1937.

1104 ELTON, William. "*Johan Johan* and Its Debt to French Farce." *JEGP*, 53 (1954), 271–2. **Cf. 1113.**

1105 GRAVES, Thornton S. "The Heywood Circle and the Reformation." *MP*, 10 (1912), 553–72.

1106 GRAVES, Thornton S. "On the Reputation of John Heywood." *MP*, 21 (1922), 209–13.

1107 HILLEBRAND, H. N. "On the Interludes Attributed to John Heywood." *MP*, 13 (1915), 267–80.

1108 JOHNSON, Robert C. *John Heywood*. New York: Twayne, 1970.

1109 MAXWELL, Ian. *French Farce and John Heywood*. Melbourne: University of Melbourne Press, 1946.

1110 MILLER, Edwin Shephard. "Guilt and Penalty in Heywood's Pardoner's Lie." *MLQ*, 10 (1949), 58–60.

1111 PHY, Wesley. "The Chronology of John Heywood's Plays." *Englische Studien,* 74 (1940), 589–91.

1112 SULTAN, Stanley. "The Audience Participation Episode in *Johan, Johan.*" *JEGP*, 52 (1953), 491–7.

1113 SULTAN, Stanley. "*Johan Johan* and Its Debt to French Farce." *JEGP,* 53 (1954), 23–37. Cf. **1104.**

1114 WITHINGTON, Robert. "Paranomasia in John Heywood's Plays." *Smith College Studies in Modern Languages,* 21 (1939–40).

1115 YOUNG, Karl. "The Influence of French Farce Upon the Plays of John Heywood." *MP,* 2 (1904), 1–28.

Heywood, Thomas (ca. 1574–1641)

Bibliography

1116 DONOVAN, ed. **See 926.**

Works

1117 *The Dramatic Works of Thomas Heywood*. 6 vols. R. H. Shepherd, ed. London: John Pearson, 1874. Reprinted, New York: Russell & Russell, 1964.

1118 *The Fair Maid of the West, Parts I and II*. Robert K. Turner, ed. Regents Renaissance Drama Series. Lincoln: University of Nebraska Press, 1969.

1119 *A Woman Killed with Kindness*. R. W. Van Fossen, ed. Revels Plays. Cambridge: Harvard University Press, 1961.

Studies

1120 BERRY, Lloyd E. "A Note on Heywood's *A Woman Killed with Kindness.*" *MLR,* 58 (1963), 64–5.

1121 BESCOU, Yves. "Thomas Heywood et le probleme de l'adultère dans *Une Femme tuée par la bonté.*" *Revue Anglo-americaine,* 9 (1931), 127–40.

1122 BESCOU, Yves. "Thomas Heywood et la sorcellerie." *Revue l'enseignement des langues vivantes,* 49 (1932).

1123 BESCOU, Yves. "Thomas Heywood et la Bourgeousie de la Renaissance anglaise." *Revue de l'enseignement des langues vivantes* (1933).

1124 BOAS, F. S. *Thomas Heywood*. London: Williams & Norgate, 1950.

1125 BROWN, Arthur. "An Edition of the Plays of Thomas Heywood: A Preliminary Survey of Problems." *RenP 1954*, (1955), 71–6.

1126 BROWN, Arthur. "Thomas Heywood's Dramatic Art." *Essays on Shakespeare and Elizabethan Drama* Pp. 327–40. **See 287.**

1127 BROWN, Arthur. "Two Notes on Thomas Heywood." *MLR*, 50 (1955), 497–8.

1128 BRYAN, Margaret B. "Food Symbolism in *A Woman Killed with Kindness.*" *HLQ*, 37 (1974), 111–22.

1129 CANUTESON, John. "The Theme of Forgiveness in the Plot and Sub-Plot of *A Woman Killed with Kindness.*" *RenD*, n.s. 2 (1969), 123–41.

1130 CLARK, Arthur M. *Thomas Heywood, Playwright and Miscellanist.* Oxford: Basil Blackwell, 1931.

1131 COOK, David. "*A Woman Killed with Kindness:* An Unshakespearian Tragedy." *ES*, 45 (1964), 353–72.

1132 COURSEN, Herbert R., Jr. "The Subplot of *A Woman Killed with Kindness.*" *ELN*, 2 (1965), 180–5.

1133 CROMWELL, Otelia. *Thomas Heywood, A Study in the Elizabethan Drama of Everyday Life.* New Haven: Yale University Press, 1928.

1134 GALINSKY, Hans. *Die Familie im Drama von Thomas Heywood.* Breslau: Priebatsch, 1936.

1135 GIORDANO-ORISINI, G. N. "Thomas Heywood's Play on 'The Troubles of Queen Elizabeth.' " *The Library*, n.s. 14 (1933), 313–38.

1136 GRIVELET, Michel. "Note sur Thomas Heywood et le Théâtre sous Charles Ier." *EA*, 7 (1954), 101–6.

1137 GRIVELET, Michel. "The Simplicity of Thomas Heywood." *SS, 14 (1961)*, 56–65.

1138 GRIVELET, Michel. *Thomas Heywood et lè drame domestique élizabéthain.* Paris: Didier, 1957.

1139 HALSTEAD, W. L. "Dekker's 'Cupid and Psyche' and Thomas Heywood." *ELH*, 11 (1944), 182–91.

1140 HOLADAY, Allan. "Heywood's *Troia Britannica* and the *Ages.*" *JEGP*, 45 (1946), 430–9.

1141 HOLADAY, Allan. "Robert Browne and the Date of Heywood's *Lucrece.*" *JEGP*, 44 (1945), 171–80.

1142 HOLADAY, Allan. "Thomas Heywood and the Puritans." *JEGP*, 49 (1950), 192–203.

1143 HOOPER, Gifford. "Heywood's *A Woman Killed with Kindness* Scene xiv: Sir Charles's Plan." *ELN*, 11 (1973), 181–8.

1144 JOHNSON, Marilyn L. *Images of Women in the Works of Thomas Heywood.* Jacobean Drama Studies 42. Salzburg: Institut für Englische Sprache und Literatur, Universität Salzburg, 1974.

1145 JOHNSTON, George Burke. "The Lute Speech in *A Woman Killed with Kindness.*" *N&QH*, n.s. 5 (1958), 525–6.

1146 McNEIR, Waldo F. "Heywood's Sources for the Main Plot of *A Woman Killed with Kindness.*" *Studies in the English Renaissance Drama.* Pp. 189–211. **See 270.**

1147 MARTIN, Robert Grant. "The Sources of Heywood's *If You Know Not Me, You Know Nobody, Part I.*" *MLN,* 39 (1924). 220–2.

1148 PATRIDES, C. A. "Thomas Heywood and Literary Piracy." *PQ,* 39 (1960), 118–22.

1149 PATTERSON, McEvoy. "Origin of the Main Plot of *A Woman Killed with Kindness.*" *UTSE,* 17 (1937), 75–87.

1150 POLLIN, Burton R. " 'Alastors' in the Works of Coryatt, Heywood, Southey, and Shelley." *ES,* 55 (1974), 428–34.

1151 RABKIN, Norman. "Dramatic Deception in Heywood's *The English Traveller.*" *SEL,* 1 (1961), 1–16.

1152 RICE, Warner G. "The Moroccan Episode in Thomas Heywood's *The Fair Maid of the West.*" *PQ,* 9 (1930), 431–40.

1153 SMITH, Hallett. "*A Woman Killed with Kindness.*" *PMLA,* 53 (1939), 138–47.

1154 SPACKS, Patricia Meyer. "Honor and Perception in *A Woman Killed with Kindness.*" *MLQ,* 20 (1959), 321–32.

1155 TOWNSEND, Freda L. "The Artistry of Thomas Heywood's Double Plots." *PQ,* 25 (1946), 97–119.

1156 URE, Peter. "Marriage and the Domestic Drama in Heywood and Ford." *ES,* 32 (1951), 200–16.

1157 WAITH, Eugene M. "Heywood's Women Worthies." *Concepts of the Hero in the Middle Ages and the Renaissance.* Albany: State University of New York Press, 1975. Pp. 22–38.

1158 WRIGHT, Louis B. "Heywood and the Popularizing of History." *MLN,* 43 (1928), 287–93.

1159 WRIGHT, Louis B. "The Male Friendship Cult in Thomas Heywood's Plays." *MLN,* 42 (1927), 510–14.

Jonson, Ben (1573?–1637)

Bibliography

1160 GUFFEY, George R., ed. *Robert Herrick, 1949–1965; Ben Jonson, 1947–1965; Thomas Randolph, 1949–1965.* Elizabethan Bibliographies Supplements 3. London: Nether Press, 1968.

Works

1161 *Ben Jonson.* 11 vols. C. H. Herford, Percy and Evelyn Simpson, eds. Oxford: The Clarendon Press, 1925–52.

1162 *Five Plays.* New York: Oxford University Press, 1953.

1163 *Ben Jonson: The Complete Masques.* Stephen Orgel, ed. New Haven: Yale University Press, 1969.

1164 *Ben Jonson: Selected Masques.* Stephen Orgel, ed. New Haven: Yale University Press, 1970.

1165 *The Alchemist.* D. Brown, ed. New Mermaids. New York: Hill & Wang, 1966.

1166 *The Alchemist.* Alvin Kernan, ed. New Haven: Yale University Press, 1974.

1167 *The Alchemist.* Francis Hugh Mares, ed. Revels Plays. Cambridge: Harvard University Press, 1967.

1168 *The Alchemist.* S. Musgrove, ed. Fountainwell. Berkeley: University of California Press, 1968.

1169 *The Alchemist.* J. B. Steane, ed. Cambridge: Cambridge University Press, 1967.

1170 *Bartholomew Fair.* E. A. Horsman, ed. Revels Plays. Cambridge: Harvard University Press, 1960.

1171 *Bartholomew Fair.* Edward B. Partridge, ed. Regents Renaissance Drama Series. Lincoln: University of Nebraska Press, 1964.

1172 *Bartholomew Fair.* Eugene M. Waith, ed. New Haven: Yale University Press, 1963.

1173 *Epicoene or the Silent Woman.* L. Beaurline, ed. Regents Renaissance Drama Series. Lincoln: University of Nebraska Press, 1966.

1174 *Epicoene or the Silent Woman.* Edward B. Partridge, ed. New Haven: Yale University Press, 1971.

1175 *Every Man in his Humour.* G. B. Jackson, ed. New Haven: Yale University Press, 1969.

1176 *Every Man in his Humour. A Parallel-Text Edition of the 1601 Quarto and the 1616 Folio.* J. W. Lever, ed. Regents Renaissance Drama Series. Lincoln: University of Nebraska Press, 1971.

1177 *Every Man in his Humour.* M. Seymour-Smith, ed. New Mermaids. New York: Hill & Wang, 1968.

1178 *Sejanus.* Jonas Barish, ed. New Haven: Yale University Press, 1965.

1179 *Sejanus.* W. F. Bolton, ed. New Mermaids. New York: Hill & Wang, 1966.

1180 *The Staple of News.* Devra Rowland Kifer, ed. Regents Renaissance Drama Series. Lincoln: University of Nebraska Press, 1975.

1181 *Volpone.* P. Brockbank, ed. New Mermaids. New York: Hill & Wang, 1968.

1182 *Volpone.* J. Halio, ed. Fountainwell. Berkeley: University of California Press, 1968.

1183 *Volpone.* Alvin Kernan, ed. New Haven: Yale University Press, 1962.

Studies

1184 ADAMS, Joseph Quincy. "*Eastward Hoe* and Its Satire Against the Scots." *SP,* 28 (1931), 689–701.

1185 ADAMS, Joseph Quincy. "The Sources of Ben Jonson's *Volpone.*" *MP,* 2 (1904), 289-99 289–99.

1186 ALLEN, Don Cameron. "Ben Jonson and the Hieroglyphics." *PQ,* 18 (1939), 290–300.

1187 ANDERSON, Mark A. "Structure and Response in *Volpone.*" *RMS,* 19 (1975), 47–71.

1188 ANDERSON, Mark A. "The Successful Unity of *Epicoene:* A Defense of Ben Jonson." *SEL,* 10 (1970), 349–66.

1189 ARMSTRONG, William A. "Ben Jonson and Jacobean Stagecraft." *Jacobean Theatre.* Pp. 43–62. **See 276.**

1190 ARNOLD, Judd. "The Double Plot in *Volpone:* A Note on Jonsonian Dramatic Structure." *17th Century Newsletter,* 23 (1965), 47–8; 50–2.

1191 ARNOLD, Judd. *A Grace Peculiar: Ben Jonson's Cavalier Heroes.* University Park: Pennsylvania State University Press, 1972.

1192 ARNOLD, Judd. "Lovewit's Triumph and Jonsonian Morality: A Reading of *The Alchemist.*" *Criticism,* 11 (1969), 151–66.

1193 BACON, Wallace A. "The Magnetic Field: The Structure of Jonson's Comedies." *HLQ,* 19 (1956), 121-53.

1194 BAMBOROUGH, J. B. *Ben Jonson.* New York: Longmans, Green, 1959.

1195 BARISH, Jonas. "Baroque Prose in the Theater: Ben Jonson." *PMLA,* 73 (1958), 184-95.

1196 BARISH, Jonas. *Ben Jonson and the Language of Prose Comedy.* Cambridge: Harvard University Press, 1960.

1197 BARISH, Jonas. "The Double Plot in *Volpone.* ` *MP,* 51 (1953), 83–92.

1198 BARISH, Jonas. "Feasting and Judging in Jonsonian Comedy." *RenD,* n.s. 5 (1972), 3–35.

1199 BARISH, Jonas. "Jonson and the Loathèd Stage." *A Celebration of Ben Jonson.* Pp. 27–53. **See 1207.**

1200 BARISH, Jonas. "Ovid, Juvenal, and The *Silent Woman.*" *PMLA,* 71 (1956), 213–24.

1201 BARISH, Jonas, ed. *Ben Jonson: A Collection of Critical Essays.* Englewood Cliffs, N.J.: Prentice-Hall, 1963.

1202 BASKERVILL, Charles R. *English Elements in Jonson's Early Comedy.* Austin: University of Texas Press, 1911.

1203 BAUM, Helena Watts. *The Satiric and Didactic in Ben Jonson's Comedy.* Chapel Hill: University of North Carolina Press, 1947.

1204 BEAURLINE, L. A. "Ben Jonson and the Illusion of Completeness." *PMLA,* 84 (1969), 51–9.

1205 BENTLEY, Gerald Eades. *Shakespeare and Jonson: Their Reputations in the Seventeenth Century Compared.* Chicago: University of Chicago Press, 1945.

1206 BERRINGER, Ralph W. "Jonson's *Cynthia's Revels* and the War of the Theatres." *PQ,* 22 (1943), 1–22.

1207 BLISSET, William, Julian PATRICK, and R. W. Van FOSSEN, eds. *A Celebration of Ben Jonson.* Toronto: University of Toronto Press, 1973.

1208 BLISSET, William. "The Venter Tripartite in *The Alchemist.*" *SEL,* 8 (1968), 323–34.

1209 BLISSET, William. "Your Majesty Is Welcome to a Fair." *The Elizabethan Theatre IV.* Pp. 80–105. **See 285.**

1210 BOUGHNER, Daniel C. *The Devil's Disciple: Ben Jonson's Debt to Machiavelli.* New York: Philosophical Library, 1968.

1211 BOUGHNER, Daniel C. "Jonson's Use of Lipsius in *Sejanus.*" *MLN,* 73 (1958), 247–55.

1212 BOUGHNER, Daniel C. "Juvenal, Horace and *Sejanus.*" *MLN,* 75 (1960), 545–50.

1213 BOUGHNER, Daniel C. "*Sejanus* and Machiavelli." *SEL,* 1 (1961) 81–100.

1214 BOWERS, Fredson T. "Ben Jonson the Actor." *SP,* 34 (1937), 392-406.

1215 BRADBROOK, M. C. "The Nature of Theatrical Experience in Ben Jonson with Special Reference to the Masques" in *Expression, Communication and Experience in Literature and Language.* London: *MHRA,* 1973. Pp. 103–17.

1216 BRADLEY, J. F., and Joseph Quincy ADAMS. *The Jonson Allusion-Book.* New Haven: Yale University Press, 1922.

1217 BRYANT, J. A., Jr. "*Catiline* and the Nature of Jonson's Tragic Fable." *PMLA,* 69 (1954), 265–77.

1218 BRYANT, J. A., Jr. *The Compassionate Satirist: Ben Jonson and His Imperfect World.* Athens: University of Georgia Press, 1973.

1219 BRYANT, J. A., Jr. "Jonson's Revision of *Every Man in His Humour.*" *SP,* 59 (1962), 641–50.

1220 BRYANT, J. A., Jr. "The Significance of Ben Jonson's First Requirement for Tragedy: 'Truth of Argument.' " *SP,* 49 (1952), 195–213.

1221 BRYANT, J. A., Jr. "*A Tale of a Tub:* Jonson's Comedy of the Human Condition." *RenP 1963,* (1964), 95–105.

1222 BURELL, Francis. "Ben Jonson." *Empire Review* (October, 1925), 392–6.

1223 BURTON, K. M. "The Political Tragedies of Chapman and Ben Jonson." *EIC,* 2 (1952), 397–412.

1224 CAMPBELL, Oscar James. "The Dramatic Construction of *Poetaster.*" *HLB,* 9 (1936), 37–62.

1225 CAMPBELL, Oscar James. "The Relation of *Epicoene* to Aretino's 'Il Marescalco.' " *PMLA,* 46 (1931), 752–62.

1226 CASTELAIN, Maurice. *Ben Jonson: l'homme et l'oeuvre.* Paris: Hachette, 1907.

1227 CHAMPION, Larry S. *Ben Jonson's "Dotages."* Lexington: University of Kentucky Press, 1967.

1228 CHUTE, Marchette. *Ben Jonson of Westminster.* New York: Dutton, 1953.

1229 CLARY, Frank N., Jr. "The Vol and the Pone: A Re-consideration of Jonson's *Volpone.*" *ELN,* 10 (1972), 102–9.

1230 COLLEY, John Scott. "Opinion, Poetry, and Folly in *Every Man in His Humour.*" *SAB,* 39, iv(1974), 3–9.

1231 COPE, Jackson I. "*Bartholomew Fair* as Blasphemy." *RenD,* 8 (1965), 127–52.

1232 COX, Gerard H., III. "Celia, Bonario, and Jonson's Indebtedness to the Medieval Cycles." *EA,* 25 (1972), 506–11.

1233 CREASER, John. "*Volpone: The Mortifying of the Fox.*" *EIC,* 25 (1975), 329–56.

1234 CREWS, Jonathan V. "Death in Venice: A Study of *Othello* and *Volpone.*" *University of Capetown Studies in English,* 4 (1973), 17–29.

1235 CUNNINGHAM, Dolora. "The Jonsonian Masque as a Literary Form." *ELH,* 22 (1955), 108–24.

1236 DAVIS, Joe Lee. *The Sons of Ben: Jonsonian Comedy in Caroline England.* Detroit: Wayne State University Press, 1967.

1237 DAVISON, P. H. "*Volpone* and the Old Comedy." *MLQ,* 24 (1963), 151–7.

1238 DeLUNA, B. N. *Jonson's Romish Plot.* Oxford: The Clarendon Press, 1967.

1239 DESSEN, Alan C. "*The Alchemist:* Jonson's 'Estates' Play." *RenD,* 7 (1964), 350–4.

1240 DESSEN, Alan C. *Jonson's Moral Comedy.* Evanston, Ill: Northwestern University Press, 1971.

1241 DESSEN, Alan C. "*Volpone* and the Late Morality Tradition." *MLQ,* 25 (1964), 388–99.

1242 DeVILLIERS, J. I. "Ben Jonson's Tragedies." *ES,* 45 (1964), 433–42.

1243 DICK, Aliki L. *Paedeia Through Laughter: Jonson's Aristophanic Appeal to Human Intelligence.* Studies in English Literature 76. The Hague: Mouton, 1974.

1244 DONALDSON, Ian. "Jonson's Tortoise." *RES,* 19 (1968), 162–6.

1245 DONALDSON, Ian. "Language, Noise and Nonsense: *The Alchemist.*" *17th Century Imagery: Essays on the Uses of Figurative Language from Donne to Farquhar.* Berkeley: University of California Press, 1971. Pp. 69–82.

1246 DONALDSON, Ian. " 'A Martyr's Resolution': Jonson's *Epicoene.*" *RES,* 18 (1967), 1–15.

1247 DONALDSON, Ian. "*Volpone*—Quick and Dead." *EIC,* 21 (1971), 121–34.

1248 DONALDSON, Ian. *The World Upside-Down: Comedy from Jonson to Fielding.* Oxford: The Clarendon Press, 1970.

1249 DORENKAMP, Angela G. "Jonson's *Catiline:* History as the Trying Faculty." *SP,* 67 (1970), 210–20.

1250 DREW-BEAR, Annette. *Rhetoric in Ben Jonson's Middle Plays: A Study of Ethics, Character Portrayal, and Persuasion.* Jacobean Drama Studies 24. Salzburg: Institut für Englische Sprache und Literatur, Universität Salzburg, 1973.

1251 DUFFY, Ellen M. T. "Ben Jonson's Debt to Renaissance Scholarship in *Sejanus* and *Catiline.*" *MLR,* 42 (1947), 24–30.

1252 DUNCAN, Douglas. "Audience-Manipulation in *Volpone.*" *Wascana Review,* 5 (1970), 23–37.

1253 DUNCAN, Douglas. "Ben Jonson's Lucianic Irony." *Ariele,* 1 (1970), 42–53.

1254 DUNCAN, Douglas. "A Guide to *The New Inn.*" *EIC,* 20 (1970), 311–26.

1255 DUNCAN, Edgar Hill. "The Alchemy in Jonson's *Mercury Vindicated.*" *SP,* 39 (1942), 625–37.

1256 DUNCAN, Edgar Hill. "Jonson's *Alchemist* and the Literature of Alchemy." *PMLA,* 61 (1946), 699–710.

1257 DUNN, Esther Cloudman. *Ben Jonson's Art: Elizabethan Life and Literature as Reflected Therein.* Northampton, Mass.: Smith College, 1925.

1258 DUTTON, A. Richard. "The Significance of Jonson's Revision of *EMI.*" *MLR,* 69 (1974), 241–9.

1259 DUTTON, A. Richard. "*Volpone* and *The Alchemist:* A Comparison in Satiric Techniques." *RMS,* 18 (1974), 36–62.

1260 ECCLES, Mark. "Jonson and the Spies." *RES,* 13 (1937), 385–97.

1261   ECHERUO, Michael J. C. "The Conscience of Politics and Jonson's *Catiline.*" *SEL,* 6 (1966), 341–56.

1262   EMPSON, William. "*Volpone.*" *Hudson Review,* 21 (1968–69), 651–66.

1263   ENCK, John J. "*The Case is Altered:* Initial Comedy of Humours." *SP,* 50 (1953), 195–214.

1264   ENCK, John J. *Jonson and the Comic Truth.* Madison: University of Wisconsin Press, 1957.

1265   ESDAILE, Katherine A. "Ben Jonson and the Devil Tavern." *E&S,* 29 (1944), 93–100.

1266   EVANS, K. W. "*Sejanus* and the Ideal Prince Tradition." *SEL,* 11 (1971), 249–64.

1267   EVANS, Willa McClung. *Ben Jonson and Elizabethan Music.* Lancaster, Penn.: Lancaster Press, 1929.

1268   FERNS, John. "Ovid, Juvenal, and the *Silent Woman:* A Reconsideration." *MLR,* 65 (1970), 248–53.

1269   FURNISS, W. Todd. "The Annotation of Ben Jonson's *Masque of Queenes.*" *RES,* 5 (1954), 344–60.

1270   FURNISS, W. Todd. "Ben Jonson's Masques." *Three Studies in the Renaissance: Sidney, Jonson, Milton.* New Haven: Yale University Press, 1958. Pp. 89–179.

1271   FURNISS, W. Todd. "Jonson's Antimasques." *RN,* 7 (1954), 21–2.

1272   GARDINER, Judith K. "Infantile Sexuality, Adult Critics, and *Bartholomew Fair.*" *L&P,* 24 (1974), 124–32.

1273   GIANAKARIS, C. J. "Identifying Ethical Values in *Volpone.*" *HLQ,* 32 (1968), 45–57.

1274   GIANAKARIS, C. J. "Jonson's Use of 'Avocatori' in *Volpone.*" *ELN,* 12 (1974), 8–14.

1275   GIBBONS, Brian. See **642.**

1276   GILBERT, Allan H. "The Eavesdropper in Jonson's *Sejanus.*" *MLN,* 69 (1954), 164–6.

1277   GILBERT, Allan H. "The Function of the Masques in *Cynthia's Revels.*" *PQ,* 22 (1943), 211–30.

1278   GILBERT, Allan H. *The Symbolic Persons in the Masques of Ben Jonson.* Durham, N.C.: Duke University Press, 1948.

1279   GOLDBERG, S. L. "Folly into Crime: The Catastrophe of *Volpone.*" *MLQ,* 20 (1959), 233–42.

1280   GORDON, D. J. "Ben Jonson's *Haddington Masque:* The Story and the Fable." *MLR,* 42 (1947), 180–7.

1281   GRAVES, Thornton S. "Jonson in the Jest Books." *Manly Anniversary Studies in Language and Literature.* Pp. 127–39. See **219.**

1282   GRAY, Henry David. "The Chamberlain's Men and the *Poetaster.*" *MLR,* 42 (1947), 173–9.

1283   GREENE, Thomas M. "Ben Jonson and the Centered Self." *SEL,* 10 (1970), 325–48.

1284 GREG, W. W. "Jonson's Masques—Points of Editorial Principle and Practice." *RES,* 19 (1942), 144–66.

1285 GREG, W. W., ed. *Jonson's Masque of Gipsies: An Attempt at a Reconstruction.* London: The British Academy, 1952.

1286 GUM, Coburn. *The Aristophanic Comedies of Ben Jonson.* The Hague: Mouton, 1967.

1287 HALLETT, Charles A. "Jonson's Celia: A Reinterpretation of *Volpone.*" *SP,* 68 (1971), 50–69.

1288 HALLETT, Charles A. "The Satanic Nature of *Volpone.*" *PQ,* 49 (1970), 41–55.

1289 HAMEL, Guy. "Order and Judgement in *Bartholomew Fair.*" *UTQ,* 43 (1973), 48–67.

1290 HAMILTON, Gary D. "Folly, Incurable Diseases, and *Volpone.*" *SEL,* 8 (1968), 335–48.

1291 HAMILTON, Gary D. "Irony and Fortune in *Sejanus.*" *SEL,* 11 (1971), 265–81.

1292 HAWKINS, Harriett. "The Idea of a Theater in Jonson's *The New Inn.*" *RenD,* 9 (1966), 205–26.

1293 HEFFNER, R. L., Jr. "Unifying Symbols in the Comedy of Ben Jonson." English Institute Essays, 1954. New York: Columbia University Press, 1955.

1294 HIBBARD, G. R. "Ben Jonson and Human Nature." *A Celebration of Ben Jonson.* Pp. 55–81. See 1207.

1295 HIBBARD, G. R. "Goodness and Greatness: An Essay on the Tragedies of Ben Jonson and George Chapman." *RMS,* 11 (1967), 5–54.

1296 HILL, Geoffrey. "The World's Proportion: Jonson's Dramatic Poetry in *Sejanus* and *Catiline.*" *Jacobean Theatre.* Pp. 113–32. See 276.

1297 HILL, W. Speed. "Biography, Autobiography, and *Volpone.*" *SEL,* 12 (1972), 309–28.

1298 HOLLWAY, Morag. "Jonson's 'Proper Straine.'" *CR,* 13 (1970), 51–67.

1299 HONIG, E. "*Sejanus* and *Coriolanus:* A Study in Alienation." *MLQ,* 12 (1951), 407–21.

1300 HOOPER, Edith S. "The Text of Ben Jonson." *MLR,* 12 (1917), 350–2.

1301 HUFFMAN, Clifford C. *"Coriolanus" in Context.* Lewisburg, Pa.: Bucknell University Press, 1972. Pp. 54–60, 223–29.

1302 HUSSEY, Maurice. "Ananias the Deacon. A Study of Religion in Jonson's *The Alchemist.*" *English,* 9 (1953), 207–12.

1303 JACKSON, G. B. *Vision and Judgment in Ben Jonson's Drama.* New Haven: Yale University Press, 1968.

1304 JANICKA, Irena. "Figurative Language in *Bartholomew Fair.*" *Shakespeare-Jahrbuch (Weimar)* (1975), 156–67.

1305 JANICKA, Irena. "The Popular Background of Ben Jonson's Masques." *ShJ,* 105 (1969), 183–208.

1306 JOHANSON, B. *Law and Lawyers in Elizabethan England as Evidenced in the Plays of Ben Jonson and Thomas Middleton.* Stockholm: Stockholm Studies in English, 1967.

1307 JOHANSON, B. *Religion and Superstition in the Plays of Ben Jonson and Thomas Middleton.* Upsala: Lundeguistska, 1950.

1308 JONES, Myrddin. "Sir Epicure Mammon: A Study in 'Spiritual Fornication.' " *RenQ,* 22 (1969), 233–42.

1309 KAPLAN, Joel H. "Dramatic and Moral Energy in Ben Jonson's *Bartholomew Fair.*" *RenD,* n.s. 3 (1970), 137–56.

1310 KAY, W. David. "The Shaping of Ben Jonson's Career: A Reexamination of Facts and Problems." *MP,* 68 (1970), 224–37.

1311 KELLICH, Martin. "Unity of Time in *Every Man in His Humour* and *Cynthia's Revels.*" *MLN,* 57 (1942), 445–9.

1312 KIFER, Devra Rowland. "The Staple of News: Jonson's Festive Comedy." *SEL,* 12 (1972), 329–44.

1313 KNIGHTS, L. C. "Ben Jonson: Public Attitudes and Social Poetry." *A Celebration of Ben Jonson.* Pp. 167–87. **See 1207.**

1314 KNOLL, Robert E. *Ben Jonson's Plays: An Introduction.* Lincoln: University of Nebraska Press, 1964.

1315 KNOLL, Robert E. "How to Read *The Alchemist.*" *CE,* 21 (1960), 456–60.

1315A KNOWLTON, Edgar C. "The Plots of Ben Jonson's Plays." *MLN,* 44 (1929), 77–86.

1316 LATHAM, Jacqueline E. M. "Form in *Bartholomew Fair.*" *English,* 21 (1972), 8–11.

1317 LEECH, Clifford. "Caroline Echoes of *The Alchemist.*" *RES,* 16 (1940), 432–8.

1318 LEECH, Clifford. "The Incredibility of Jonsonian Comedy." *A Celebration of Ben Jonson.* Pp. 3–25. **See 1207.**

1319 LEGGATT, Alexander. "The Suicide of *Volpone.*" *UTQ,* 39 (1969), 19–32.

1320 LEVIN, Harry. "Jonson's Metempsychosis." *PQ,* 22 (1943), 231–9.

1321 LEVIN, Lawrence L. "Clement Justice in *Every Man in His Humour.*" *SEL,* 12 (1972), 291–307.

1322 LEVIN, Lawrence L. "Justice and Society in *Sejanus* and *Volpone.*" *Discourse,* 13 (1970), 319–24.

1323 LEVIN, Lawrence L. "Replication as Dramatic Strategy in the Comedies of Ben Jonson." *RenD,* n.s. 5 (1972), 37–74.

1324 LEVIN, Richard. "The New *New Inn* and the Proliferation of Good Bad Drama." *EIC,* 22 (1972), 41–7.

1325 LEVIN, Richard. "The Structure of *Bartholomew Fair.*" *PMLA,* 80 (1965), 172–9.

1326 LINDSAY, Edwin S. "The Music in Ben Jonson's Plays." *MLN,* 44 (1929), 86–92.

1327 LINKLATER, Eric. *Ben Jonson and King James: A Biography and a Portrait.* London: Cape, 1931.

1328 LITT, Dorothy. "Unity of Theme in *Volpone.*" *BNYPL,* 73 (1969), 218–26.

1329 LYLE, Alexander W. "Volpone's Two Worlds." *YES,* 4 (1974), 70–6.

1330 McCULLEN, Joseph T., Jr. "Conference with the Queen of Fairies: A Study of Jonson's Workmanship in *The Alchemist.*" *Studia Neophilologica,* 23 (1951), 87–95.

1331 McEUEN, Kathryn Anderson. *Classical Influence Upon the Tribe of Ben.* Cedar Rapids, Iowa: Torch Press, 1939.

1332 McFARLAND, Ronald E. "Jonson's *Magnetic Lady* and the Reception of Gilbert's De Magnete." *SEL,* 11 (1971), 283–93.

1333 McGALLIARD, John C. "Chaucerian Comedy: The *Merchant's Tale,* Jonson, and Molière." *PQ,* 25 (1946), 343–70.

1334 McKENZIE, Donald F. " 'The Staple of News' and the Late Plays." *A Celebration of Ben Jonson.* Pp. 83–128. See 1207.

1335 McPHARLIN, Paul. "Ben Jonson: Inigo Jones: Inventors." *Mask,* 12 (1927), 10–4.

1336 McPHERSON, David. "Some Renaissance Sources for Jonson's Early Comic Theory." *ELN,* 8 (1971), 180–2.

1337 MAROTTI, Arthur F. "The Self-Reflexive Act of Ben Jonson's *Sejanus.*" *TSLL,* 12 (1970), 197–220.

1338 MEAGHER, John C. *Method and Meaning in Jonson's Masques.* Notre Dame: University of Notre Dame Press, 1966.

1339 MILLS, Lloyd. "Barish's 'The Double Plot' Supplemented: The Tortoise Symbolism." *Serif,* 4 (1967), 25–8.

1340 MUSGROVE, S. *Shakespeare and Jonson.* Auckland: Auckland University College, 1957.

1341 NAKANO, Yoshio. "Ben Jonson's Comedy." *Studies in English Literature, Imperial University of Tokyo,* 9 (1929), 256–75.

1342 NASH, Ralph. "The Comic Intent of *Volpone.*" *SP,* 44 (1947), 26–40.

1343 NASH, Ralph. "The Parting Scene in Jonson's *Poetaster* (IV, ix)." *PQ,* 31 (1952), 54–62.

1344 NASON, Arthur. *Heralds and Heraldry in Ben Jonson's Plays, Masques and Entertainments.* New York: New York University Press, 1907.

1345 NOYES, Robert Gale. *Ben Jonson on the English Stage, 1660–1774.* Cambridge: Harvard University Press, 1935.

1346 OLIVE, W. J. "*Sejanus* and *Hamlet.*" *A Tribute to George Coffin Taylor.* Chapel Hill: University of North Carolina Press, 1952. Pp. 178–84.

1347 ORGEL, Stephen. *The Jonsonian Masque.* Cambridge: Harvard University Press, 1965.

1348 PALMER, John. *Ben Jonson.* New York: Viking Press, 1934.

1349 PARFITT, G. A. E. "Some Notes on the Classical Borrowings in *Volpone.*" *ES,* 55 (1974), 127–32.

1350 PARKER, R. B. "The Themes and Staging of *Bartholomew Fair.*" *UTQ,* 39 (1970), 293–309.

1351 PARR, Johnstone. "Non-Alchemical Pseudo-Sciences in *The Alchemist.*" *PQ,* 24 (1945), 85–9.

1352 PARROTT, T. M. "Comedy in the Court Masque: A Study of Jonson's Contributions." *Renaissance Studies in Honor of Hardin Craig.* Stanford: Stanford University Press, 1941. Pp. 236–49. [Also in *PQ,* 20 (1941), 428–41.]

1353 PARTRIDGE, A. C. *The Accidence of Ben Jonson's Plays, Masques, and Entertainments.* Cambridge: Bowes & Bowes, 1953.

1354 PARTRIDGE, A. C. "The Periphrastic Auxiliary Verb 'Do' and Its Use in the Plays of Ben Jonson." *MLR,* 43 (1948), 26–33.

1355 PARTRIDGE, A. C. *Studies in the Syntax of Ben Jonson's Plays.* Cambridge: Bowes & Bowes, 1953.

1356 PARTRIDGE, Edward B. "The Allusiveness of *Epicoene.*" *ELH,* 22 (1955), 93–107.

1357 PARTRIDGE, Edward B. "Ben Jonson: The Makings of the Dramatist (1596–1602)." *Elizabethan Theatre* (Stratford). Pp. 221–44. **See 277.**

1358 PARTRIDGE, Edward B. *The Broken Compass: A Study of the Major Comedies of Ben Jonson.* London: Chatto & Windus, 1958.

1359 PARTRIDGE, Edward B. "Jonson's Large and Uniques View of Life." *The Elizabethan Theatre IV.* Pp. 143–67. **See 285.**

1360 PARTRIDGE, Edward B. "The Symbolism of Clothes in Jonson's Last Plays." *JEGP,* 56 (1957), 396–409.

1361 PASTER, Gail K. "Ben Jonson and the Uses of Architecture." *RenQ,* 27 (1974), 306–320.

1362 PASTER, Gail K. "Ben Jonson's Comedy of Limitation." *SP,* 72 (1975), 51–71.

1363 PENNANEN, Esko V. *Chapters on the Language of Ben Jonson's Dramatic Works.* Annales Universitatis Turkuensis, Ser. B, 39. Turku, 1951.

1364 PERKINSON, Richard H. "*Volpone* and the Reputation of Venetian Justice." *MLR,* 35 (1940), 11–8.

1365 PETERSON, Richard S. "The Iconography of Jonson's *Pleasure Reconciled to Virtue.*" *JMRS,* 5 (1975), 123–53.

1366 PETRONELLA, Vincent F. "Jonson's *Bartholomew Fair:* A Study in Baroque Style." *Discourse,* 13 (1970), 325–37.

1367 PETRONELLA, Vincent F. "Teaching Ben Jonson's *The Alchemist.* Alchemy and Analysis." *HAB,* 21 (1970), 19–23.

1368 PINEAS, Rainer. "The Morality Vice in *Volpone.*" *Discourse,* 5 (1962), 451–9.

1369 PLATZ, Norbert H. "Jonson's *Ars Poetica:* An Interpretation of *Poetaster* in its Historical Context." *Salzburg Studies in English Literature: Elizabethan Studies.* Salzburg: Institut für Englische Sprache und Literatur, Universität Salzburg, 1973. Pp. 1–42.

1370 POTTER, John. "Old Comedy in *Bartholomew Fair.*" *Criticism,* 10 (1968), 290–9.

1371 PRAZ, Mario. "Ben Jonson." *La Cultura,* 6 (1928), 12.

1372 PUTNEY, Rufus. "Jonson's Poetic Comedy." *PQ,* 41 (1962), 188–204.

1373 REDWINE, James D., Jr. "Beyond Psychology: The Moral Basis of Jonson's Theory of Humour Characterization." *ELH,* 28 (1961), 316–34.

1374 REED, Robert R., Jr. "Ben Jonson's Pioneering in Sentimental Comedy." *N&Q,* 195 (1950), 272–3.

1375 REYNOLDS, George F. "The Dramatic Quality of Jonson's Masques." *PQ*, 22 (1943), 230–8.

1376 RICKS, Christopher. "*Sejanus* and Dismemberment." *MLN*, 76 (1961), 301–8.

1377 ROBINSON, James E. "*Bartholomew Fair:* Comedy of Vapors." *SEL*, 1 (1961), 65–80.

1378 ROLLIN, Roger B. "Images of Libertinism in *EMI* and 'To his Coy Mistress.' " *PLL*, 6 (1970), 188–91.

1379 SACKTON, Alexander H. *Rhetoric as a Dramatic Language in Ben Jonson.* New York: Columbia University Press, 1948.

1380 SACKTON, Alexander H. "The Rhymed Couplet in Ben Jonson's Plays." *UTSE*, 30 (1951), 86–106.

1381 SALINGAR, L. G. "Farce and Fashion in *The Silent Woman.*" *ES*, n.s. 20 (1967), 29–46.

1382 SAVAGE, James E. "Ben Jonson and Shakespeare: 1623–1626." *UMSE*, 10 (1969), 25–48.

1383 SCHEVE, D. A. "Jonson's *Volpone* and Traditional Fox Lore." *RES*, n.s. 1 (1950), 242–4.

1384 SCHOENBAUM, S. "The Humorous Jonson." *The Elizabethan Theatre IV.* Pp. 1–21. See **285.**

1385 SCHOENBAUM, S. "Shakespeare and Jonson: Fact and Myth." *Elizabethan Theatre II.* Pp. 1–19. See **283.**

1386 SCOUFOS, Alice L. "Nashe, Jonson, and the Oldcastle Problem." *MP*, 65 (1966), 307–24.

1387 SHAPIRO, Michael. "Audience vs. Dramatist in Jonson's *Epicoene* and Other Plays of the Children's Troupes." *ELR*, 3 (1973), 400–17.

1388 SIMMONS, J. L. "Volpone as Antinous: Jonson and 'Th' Overthrow of Stage-Playes'." *MLR*, 70 (1975), 13–9.

1389 SIMPSON, Evelyn. "Jonson and Dickens: A Study in the Comic Genius of London." *E&S*, 29 (1943), 89–92.

1390 SISSON, C. J. "A Topical Reference in *The Alchemist.*" *Joseph Quincy Adams Memorial Studies.* Pp. 739–41. See **289.**

1390A SLIGHTS, William W. E. "Epicoene and the Prose Paradox." *PQ*, 49 (1970), 178–87.

1391 SMALL, Roscoe A. *The Stage-Quarrel Between Jonson and the So-called Poetasters.* Breslau: M. & H. Marcus, 1899.

1392 SMITH, Calvin C. "*Bartholomew Fair:* Cold Decorum." *Essays in the Renaissance.* Pp. 548–56. See **290.**

1393 SNUGGS, Henry L. "The Comic Humours: A New Interpretation." *PMLA*, 62 (1947), 114–22.

1394 SPRAGUE, Arthur Colby. "*The Alchemist* on the Stage." *TN*, 17 (1963), 46–7.

1395 STEEL, Byron. *O Rare Ben Jonson.* New York: Knopf, 1927.

1396 STERNFELD, Frederic W. "Song in Jonson's Comedy: A Gloss on *Volpone.*" *Studies in the English Renaissance Drama* Pp. 310–21. See **270.**

1397 STROUD, Theodore A. "Ben Jonson and Father Thomas Wright." *ELH,* 14 (1947), 274–82.

1398 STURMBERGER, Ingeborg Maria. *The Comic Elements in Ben Jonson's Drama.* Jacobean Drama Studies 54–55. Salzburg: Institut für Englische Sprache und Literatur, Universität Salzburg, 1975.

1399 SWINBURNE, Algernon C. *A Study of Ben Jonson.* New York: Worthington, 1889.

1400 SYMONDS, J. A. *Ben Jonson.* London: Longmans, Green, 1886.

1401 SYMONS, Julian. "Ben Jonson as Social Realist: *Bartholomew Fair.*" *Southern Review,* 6 (1940), 375–86.

1402 TALBERT, Ernest W. "The Classical Mythology and the Structure of *Cynthia's Revels.*" *PQ,* 22 (1943), 193–210.

1403 TALBERT, Ernest W. "Current Scholarly Works and the 'Erudition' of Jonson's *Masque of Augurs.*" *SP,* 44 (1947), 605–24.

1404 TALBERT, Ernest W. "The Interpretation of Jonson's Courtly Spectacles." *PMLA,* 41 (1946), 454–73.

1405 TALBERT, Ernest W. "New Light on Ben Jonson's Workmanship." *SP,* 40 (1943), 154–85.

1406 TALBERT, Ernest W. "The Purpose and Technique of Jonson's *Poetaster.*" *SP,* 42 (1945), 225–52.

1407 THAYER, C. G. *Ben Jonson: Studies in the Plays.* Norman: University of Oklahoma Press, 1963.

1408 THAYER, C. G. "Theme and Structure in *The Alchemist.*" *ELH,* 26 (1959), 23–35.

1409 THRON, E. M. "Jonson's *Cynthia's Revels:* Multiplicity and Unity." *SEL,* 11 (1971), 235–47.

1410 TOWNSEND, Freda L. *Apologie for Bartholomew Fayre: The Art of Jonson's Comedies.* New York: Modern Language Association, 1947.

1411 TOWNSEND, Freda L. "Ben Jonson's 'Censure' of Rutter's *Shepheards Holy Day.*" *MP,* 44 (1947), 238–47.

1412 TULIP, James. "Comedy as Equivocation: An Approach to the Reference of *Volpone.*" *SoRA,* 5 (1972), 91–101.

1413 ULRICH, Ernst. "Die Musik in Ben Jonson's Maskenspielen und Entertainments." *ShJ,* 73 (1937), 53–84.

1414 URBAN, Raymond. "The Somerset Affair, the Belvoir Witches, and Jonson's Pastoral Comedies." *HLB,* 23 (1975), 295–323.

1415 VOCHT, Henry De. *Studies on the Texts of Ben Jonson's "Poetaster" and "Sejanus."* Materials for the Study of the Old English Drama, No. 27. Louvain: Uystprust, 1958.

1416 WAITH, Eugene M. "The Poet's Morals in Jonson's *Poetaster.*" *MLQ,* 12 (1951), 13–9.

1417 WAITH, Eugene M. "The Staging of *Bartholomew Fair.*" *SEL,* 2 (1962), 181–95.

1418 WAITH, Eugene M. "Things as They Are and the World of Absolutes in Jonson's Plays and Masques." *The Elizabethan Theatre IV.* Pp. 106–26. **See 285.**

1419 WARREN, Michael J. "The Location of Jonson's *Catiline* III, 490–754." *PQ,* 48 (1969), 561–5.

1420 WELD, John S. "Christian Comedy: *Volpone.*" *SP,* 51 (1954), 172–93.

1421 WERTHEIM, Albert. **See 2085.**

1422 WESCOTT, Robert. "Volpone? Or the Fox?" *CR,* 17 (1974), 82–96.

1423 WHEELER, Charles Francis. *Classical Mythology in the Plays, Masques and Poems of Ben Jonson.* Princeton: Princeton University Press, 1938.

1424 WILLIAMS, Mary C. "Ben Jonson's 'Apology' for *Bartholomew Fair.*" *ELN,* 10 (1973), 180–5.

1425 WILLIAMS, Mary C. *Unity in Ben Jonson's Early Comedies.* Jacobean Drama Studies 22. Salzburg: Institut für Englische Sprache und Literatur, Universität Salzburg, 1972.

1426 WITT, Robert W. *Mirror within a Mirror: Ben Jonson and the Play-within.* Jacobean Drama Studies 46. Salzburg: Institut für Englische Sprache und Literatur, Universität Salzburg, 1975.

1427 WOLF, William D. *The Reform of the Fallen World: The "Virtuous Prince" in Jonsonian Tragedy and Comedy.* Jacobean Drama Studies 27. Salzburg: Institut für Englische Sprache und Literatur, Universität Salzburg, 1973. /

1428 WOODBRIDGE, Elizabeth. *Studies in Jonson's Comedies.* New York: Lamson Wolffe, 1898.

1429 WREN, Robert M. "Ben Jonson as Producer." *ETJ,* 22 (1970), 284–90.

Kyd, Thomas (1558?–1594)

Bibliography

1430 JOHNSON, R. ed. **See 1043.**

Works

1431 *The Works of Thomas Kyd.* F. S. Boas, ed. Oxford: The Clarendon Press, 1901.

1432 *The First Part of Hieronimo* and *The Spanish Tragedy.* A. S. Cairncross, ed. Regents Renaissance Drama Series. Lincoln: University of Nebraska Press, 1967.

1433 *The Spanish Tragedy.* Philip Edwards, ed. Revels Plays. Cambridge: Harvard University Press, 1959.

1434 *The Spanish Tragedy.* Bertram Joseph, ed. New Mermaids. New York: Hill & Wang, 1964.

1435 *The Spanish Tragedy.* T. W. Ross, ed. Fountainwell. Berkeley: University of California Press, 1968.

Studies

1436 ADAMS, Barry B. "The Audiences of *The Spanish Tragedy.*" *JEGP,* 68 (1969), 221–36.

1437 BAKER, Howard. "Ghosts and Guides: Kyd's *Spanish Tragedy* and the Medieval Tragedy." *MP*, 32 (1935), 27–36.

1438 BALDWIN, T. W. "On the Chronology of Thomas Kyd's Plays." *MLN*, 40 (1925), 343–9.

1439 BALDWIN, T. W. "Thomas Kyd's Early Company Connections." *PQ*, 6 (1927), 311–3.

1440 BARISH, Jonas. "*The Spanish Tragedy*, or The Pleasures and Perils of Rhetoric." *Elizabethan Theatre* (Stratford). Pp. 59–86. **See 277.**

1441 BERCOVITCH, Sacvan. "Love and Strife in Kyd's *Spanish Tragedy*." *SEL*, 9 (1969), 215–29.

1442 BIESTERFELDT, P. W. *Die dramatische Technik Thomas Kyds*. Halle: Niemeyer, 1936.

1443 BOWERS, Fredson T. "Kyd's Pedringano: Sources and Parallels." *Harvard Studies and Notes in Philology and Literature*, 13 (1932), 241–9.

1444 BROUDE, Ronald. "Time, Truth, and Right in *The Spanish Tragedy*." *SP*, 68 (1971), 130–45.

1445 BURROWS, Ken C. "The Dramatic and Structural Significance of the Portuguese Subplot in *The Spanish Tragedy*." *RenP 1968*, (1969), 25–35.

1446 CANNON, C. K. "The Relation of the Additions of *The Spanish Tragedy* to the Original Play." *SEL*, 2 (1962), 229–39.

1447 CARRÈRE, Felix. *Le Théâtre de Thomas Kyd: Contribution à l'Étude du Drame Elizabéthain*. Toulouse: Eduard Privat, 1951.

1448 CHICKERA, Ernst De. "Divine Justice and Private Revenge in *The Spanish Tragedy*. *MLR*, 57 (1962), 228–32.

1449 COLLEY, John Scott. "*The Spanish Tragedy: A Speaking Picture*." *ELR*, 4 (1974), 203–17.

1450 COURSEN, Herbert R., Jr. "The Unity of *The Spanish Tragedy*." *SP*, 65 (1968), 768–82.

1451 EDWARDS, Philip. *Thomas Kyd and Early Elizabethan Tragedy*. Writers and Their Works Series. London: Longmans, Green, 1966.

1452 EMPSON, William. "*The Spanish Tragedy*." *Nimbus*, 3 (1956), 16–29.

1453 FABER, M. D., and Colin SKINNER. "*The Spanish Tragedy*: Act IV." *PQ*, 49 (1970), 444–59.

1454 FREEMAN, Arthur. *Thomas Kyd: Facts and Problems*. Oxford: The Clarendon Press, 1967.

1455 GRUBB, Marion. "Kyd's Borrowing from Garnier's *Bradamante*." *MLN*, 50 (1935), 169–71.

1456 HAMILTON, Donna B. "*The Spanish Tragedy: A Speaking Picture*." *ELR*, 4 (1974), 203–17.

1457 HUNTER, G. K. "Ironies of Justice in *The Spanish Tragedy*." *RenD*, 8 (1965), 89–104.

1458 JENSEN, Ejner. "Kyd's *Spanish Tragedy*: The Play Explains Itself." *JEGP*, 64 (1965), 7–16.

1459 JOHNSON, S. F. "*The Spanish Tragedy*, or Babylon Revisited." *Essays on Shakespeare and Elizabethan Drama*. Pp. 23–36. **See 287.**

1460 KISTNER, Arthur L. and M. K. KISTNER. "The Senecan Background of Despair in *The Spanish Tragedy* and *Titus Andronicus.*" *ShakS,* 7 (1974), 1–10.

1461 LAIRD, David. "Hieronimo's Dilemma." *SP,* 62 (1965), 137–46.

1462 LAMB, Margaret. "Beyond Revenge: *The Spanish Tragedy.*" *Mosaic,* 9,i(1975), 33–40.

1463 LEGATT, Alexander. "The Three Worlds of *The Spanish Tragedy.*" *SoRA,* 6 (1973), 35–47.

1464 LEVIN, Michael Henry. " 'Vindicta mihi!' Meaning, Morality, and Motivation in *The Spanish Tragedy.*" *SEL,* 4 (1964), 307–24.

1465 McMILLIN, Scott. "The Book of Seneca in *The Spanish Tragedy.*" *SEL,* 14 (1974), 201–8.

1466 McMILLIN, Scott. "The Figure of Silence in *The Spanish Tragedy.*" *ELH,* 39 (1972), 27–48.

1467 MURRAY, Peter B. *Thomas Kyd.* New York: Twayne, 1970.

1468 RATLIFF, J. D. "Hieronimo Explains Himself." *SP,* 54 (1957), 112–8.

1469 ROWAN, D. F. See 232.

1470 SMIT, Joseph de. *Thomas Kyd, l'homme, l'oeuvre, le milieu, suivi de "La Tragedie espagnole."* Brussels: La Renaissance de l'Orient, 1925.

1471 WELLS, William. "Thomas Kyd and the Chronicle-History." *N&Q,* 178 (1940), 218–24. 238–43.

1472 WIATT, William K. "The Dramatic Function of the Alexandro-Villuppo Episode in *The Spanish Tragedy.*" *N&Q,* n.s. 5 (1958), 327–9.

1473 WILLBURN, David P. "Thomas Kyd's *The Spanish Tragedy:* Inverted Vengeance." *AI,* 28 (1971), 247–67.

1474 WYLER, Siegfried. " 'Death' in Thomas Kyd's *Spanish Tragedy:* A Study of a Semantic Field." *Festschrift Rudolf Stamm* Bern: Franche, 1969. Pp. 163–87.

Lyly, John (1554?–1606)

Bibliography

1475 JOHNSON, ed. See 1052.

Works

1476 *The Complete Works of John Lyly.* R. Warwick Bond, ed. Oxford: The Clarendon Press, 1902.

1477 *Gallathea* and *Midas.* Anne Lancashire, ed. Regents Renaissance Drama Series. Lincoln: University of Nebraska Press, 1969.

1478 *Mother Bombie.* Harriette A. Andreadis, ed. Elizabethan & Renaissance Studies 35. Salzburg: Institut für Englische Sprache und Literatur, Universität Salzburg, 1975.

1479 *Mother Bombie.* Kathleen M. Lea, ed. London: Oxford University Press, 1948.

Studies

1480 BARISH, Jonas. "The Prose Style of John Lyly." *ELH,* 23 (1956), 14–35.

1481 BENNETT, J. W. "Oxford and *Endimion." PMLA,* 57 (1942), 354–69.

1482 BEST, Michael. "Lyly's Static Drama." *RenD,* n.s. 1 (1968), 75–86.

1483 BEST, Michael. "Nashe, Lyly, and *Summer's Last Will and Testament." PQ,* 48 (1969), 1–11.

1484 BEST, Michael. "A Theory of the Literary Genesis of Lyly's *Midas." RES,* 17 (1966), 133–40.

1485 BEVINGTON, David M. "John Lyly and Queen Elizabeth: Royal Flattery in *Campaspe* and *Sapho and Phao." RenP 1966,* (1967), 57–67.

1486 BOND, Sallie. "John Lyly's *Endimion." SEL,* 14 (1974), 189–200.

1487 BOUGHNER, Daniel C. "The Background of Lyly's Tophas." *PMLA,* 54 (1939), 967–73.

1488 BRYANT, J. A., Jr. "The Nature of the Allegory in Lyly's *Endimion." RenP 1956,* (1957), 4–11.

1489 CROLL, Morris W. *Style, Rhetoric, and Rhythm: Essays by Morris W. Croll.* J. Max Patrick *et al.,* eds. Princeton: Princeton University Press, 1966.

1490 DEATS, Sara. "The Disarming of the Knight: Comic Parody in Lyly's *Endymion." SAB,* 40, iv(1975), 67–75.

1491 FEUILLERAT, Albert. *John Lyly: Contribution à l'Histoire de la Renaissance en Angleterre.* Cambridge: Cambridge University Press, 1910.

1492 HILLIARD, Stephen S. "Lyly's *Midas* as an Allegory of Tyranny." *SEL,* 12 (1972), 243–58.

1493 HOTSON, Leslie, ed. *Queen Elizabeth's Entertainment at Mitcham.* By John Lyly. New Haven: Yale University Press, 1953.

1494 HUNTER, G. K. *John Lyly: The Humanist as Courtier.* London: Routledge & Kegan Paul, 1962.

1495 HUPPÉ, Bernard. "Allegory of Love in Lyly's Court Comedies." *ELH,* 14 (1947), 93–113.

1496 JEFFERY, Violet M. *John Lyly and the Italian Renaissance.* Paris: H. Champion, 1928.

1497 KING, Walter N. "John Lyly and Elizabethan Rhetoric." *SP,* 52 (1955), 149–61.

1498 KNIGHT, G. Wilson. "Lyly." *RES,* 15 (1939), 146–63.

1499 LARAPÈRE, Anne. "The Dramatic Use of the Supernatural in John Lyly's Court Comedies." *Caliban,* 10 (1974), 49–55.

1500 MINCOFF, Marco. "Shakespeare and Lyly." *SS,* 14 (1961), 15–24.

1501 MOORE, John Robert. "The Songs in Lyly's Plays." *PMLA,* 42 (1927), 623–40.

1502 PARNELL, Paul E. "Moral Allegory in Lyly's *Loves Metamorphosis." SP,* 52 (1955), 1–16.

1503 PARR, Johnstone. **See 1717.**

1504 POWELL, Jocelyn. "John Lyly and the Language of Play." *Elizabethan Theatre* (Stratford). Pp. 147–68. **See 277.**

1505 RINGLER, William. "The Immediate Source of Euphuism." *PMLA,* 52 (1938), 678–86.

1506 SACCIO, Peter. *The Court Comedies of John Lyly: A Study in Allegorical Dramaturgy.* Princeton: Princeton University Press, 1969.

1507 SACCIO, Peter. "The Oddity of Lyly's *Endimion.*" *The Elizabethan Theatre V.* Pp. 92–111. **See 286.**

1508 STEVENSON, David. *The Love Game Comedy.* New York: Columbia University Press, 1946.

1509 TILLOTSON, Geoffrey. "The Prose of Lyly's Comedies." *Essays in Criticism and Research* (1942). Reprinted Hamden, Conn.: Archon, 1967.

1510 TURNER, Robert Y. "Some Dialogues of Love in Lyly's Comedies." *ELH,* 29 (1962), 276–88.

1511 WELTNER, Peter. "The Antinomic Vision of Lyly's *Endymion.*" *ELR,* 3 (1973), 5–29.

1512 WILLCOX, Alice. "Medical References in the Dramas of John Lyly." *Annals of Medical History,* 10 (1938), 117–26.

1513 WILSON, John Dover. *John Lyly.* Cambridge: Macmillan & Bowes, 1905.

1514 WOLFF, S. L. "The Humanist as Man of Letters: John Lyly." *SR,* 31 (1923), 8–35.

Marlowe, Christopher (1564–1593)

Bibliography

1515 JOHNSON, Robert C., ed. *Christopher Marlowe, 1946–1965.* Elizabethan Bibliographies Supplements 6. London: Nether Press, 1967.

Works

1516 *The Works of Christopher Marlowe.* C. F. Tucker Brooke, ed. Oxford: The Clarendon Press, 1910.

1517 *The Works and Life of Christopher Marlowe.* 6 vols. R. H. Case, ed. London: Methuen, 1930–33. Reprinted, New York: Gordian Press, 1961.

1518 *The Complete Works of Christopher Marlowe.* 2 vols. Fredson T. bowers, ed. Cambridge: Cambridge University Press, 1973.

1519 *The Complete Plays of Christopher Marlowe.* Irving Ribner, ed. New York: The Odyssey Press, 1963.

1520 *The Plays of Christopher Marlowe.* Leo Kirschbaum, ed. Cleveland, Ohio and New York: Meridian Books, 1962.

1521 *The Plays of Christopher Marlowe.* Roma Gill, ed. London: Oxford University Press, 1971.

1522 *Dido, Queen of Carthage* and *The Massacre at Paris.* H. J. Oliver, ed. Revels Plays. Cambridge: Harvard University Press, 1968.

1523 *Doctor Faustus.* Keith Walker, ed. Edinburgh: Oliver & Boyd, 1973.

1524 *Doctor Faustus.* Roma Gill, ed. New Mermaids. New York: Hill & Wang, 1965.

1525 *Doctor Faustus: 1604–1616. Parallel Texts.* W. W. Greg, ed. Oxford: Clarendon Press, 1950.

1526 *Christopher Marlowe's Dr. Faustus.* J. D. Jump, ed. The Revels Plays. London: Methuen, 1962.

1527 *Christopher Marlowe's Dr. Faustus: Text and Major Criticism.* Irving Ribner, ed. New York: Odyssey, 1966.

1528 *Edward II.* W. M. Merchant, ed. New Mermaids. New York: Hill & Wang, 1967.

1529 *Christopher Marlowe's Edward II: Text and Major Criticism.* Irving Ribner, ed. New York: Odyssey, 1970.

1530 *The Jew of Malta.* T. W. Craik, ed. New Mermaids. New York: Hill & Wang, 1966.

1531 *The Jew of Malta.* R. W. Van Fossen, ed. Regents Renaissance Drama Series. Lincoln: University of Nebraska Press, 1964.

1532 *Tamburlaine the Great, Parts I and II.* J. W. Harper, ed. New York: Hill & Wang, 1971.

1533 *Tamburlaine the Great, Parts I and II.* J. D. Jump, ed. Regents Renaissance Drama Series. Lincoln: University of Nebraska Press, 1967.

1534 *Christopher Marlowe's Tamburlaine Parts I and II: Text and Major Criticism.* Irving Ribner, ed. Indianapolis and New York: Odyssey, 1974.

Studies

1535 ALEXANDER, Nigel. *The Performance of Christopher Marlowe's "Dr. Faustus."* London: Oxford University Press, 1971.

1536 ALLEN, Don Cameron. "Marlowe's *Dido* and the Tradition." *Essays on Shakespeare and Elizabethan Drama.* Pp. 55–68. **See 287.**

1537 ALLEN, Don Cameron. "Renaissance Remedies for Fortune: Marlowe and the *Fortunati.*" *SP,* 38 (1941), 188–97.

1538 ARMSTRONG, William A. "*Tamburlaine* and *The Wounds of Civil War.*" *N&Q,* n.s. 5 (1958), 381–3.

1539 ATKINSON, A. D. "Marlowe and the Voyagers." *N&Q,* 194 (1949), 247–50, 273–5.

1540 BABB, Howard S. "Policy in Marlowe's *The Jew of Malta.*" *ELH,* 24 (1957), 85–94.

1541 BAKELESS, John. *Christopher Marlowe: The Man in His Time.* New York: Morrow, 1937.

1542 BAKELESS, John. *The Tragical History of Christopher Marlowe.* 2 vols. Cambridge: Harvard University Press, 1942.

1543 BARBER, C. L. "The Death of Zenocrate: 'Conceiving and Subduing Both' in Marlowe's *Tamburlaine.*" *Literature and Psychoanalysis,* 16 (1966), 13–24.

1544 BARBER, C. L. "The Form of Faustus' Fortunes Good or Bad." *TDR,* 8 (1964), 92–119.

1545 BARRINGTON, Michael. "Marlowe's Alleged Atheism." *N&Q,* 195 (1950), 260–1.

1546 BATTENHOUSE, Roy W. *Marlowe's Tamburlaine: A Study in Renaissance Moral Philosophy.* Nashville, Tenn.: Vanderbilt University Press, 1941.

1547 BATTENHOUSE, Roy W. "Protestant Apologetics and the Subplot of *2 Tamburlaine.*" *ELR,* 3 (1973), 30–43.

1548 BATTENHOUSE, Roy W. "The Relation of *Henry V* to *Tamburlaine.*" *ShakS,* 27 (1974), 71–9.

1549 BATTENHOUSE, Roy W. "Tamburlaine, the Scourge of God." *PMLA,* 56 (1941), 337–48.

1550 BAWCUTT, N. W. "Machiavelli and Marlowe's *The Jew of Malta.*" *RenD,* n.s. 3 (1970), 3–49.

1551 BENAQUIST, Lawrence M. "The Ethical Structure of *Tamburlaine, Part I.*" *Thoth,* 10 (1969), 3–19.

1552 BENAQUIST, Lawrence M. *The Tripartite Structure of Christopher Marlowe's Tamburlaine Plays and "Edward II."* Elizabethan & Renaissance Studies 43. Salzburg: Institut für Englische Sprache und Literatur, Universität Salzburg, 1975.

1553 BERDAN, John M. "Marlowe's *Edward II.*" *PQ,* 3 (1924), 197–207.

1554 BLUESTONE, Max. "*Libido Speculandi:* Doctrine and Dramaturgy in Contemporary Interpretations of Marlowe's *Doctor Faustus.*" *Reinterpretations of Elizabethan Drama.* Norman Rabkin, ed. New York: Columbia University Press, 1969. Pp. 33–88.

1555 BOAS, F. S. *Christopher Marlowe: A Biographical and Critical Study.* Oxford: The Clarendon Press, 1940.

1556 BOAS, F. S. *Marlowe and His Circle.* London: H. Milford, 1931.

1557 BOBIN, Donna. "Marlowe's Humor." *MSE,* 2 (1969), 29–40.

1558 BÖHM, Rudolph. "Die Marlowe-Forschung der letzten beiden Jahrzehute." *Anglia,* 73 (1965), 324–43.

1559 BOWERS, Fredson T. "Marlowe's *Doctor Faustus:* The 1602 Additions." *SB,* 26 (1973), 1–18.

1560 BOWERS, Fredson T. "The Text of Marlowe's *Faustus.*" *MP,* 49 (1952), 195–204.

1561 BRACHFELD, O. "Marlowe als Vorläufer der Individualpsychologie." *Internationale Zs. f. Individualpsychologie,* 6 (1929), H. 1.

1562 BREUER, Horst. "Marlowes *Der Jude von Malta.*" *Germanisch-romanische Monatsschrift, Neue Folge,* 25 (1975), 401–22.

1563 BRIGGS, William Dinsmore. "On a Document Concerning Christopher Marlowe." *SP,* 20 (1923), 153–9.

1564 BRODWIN, Leonora L. "*Edward II:* Marlowe's Culminating Treatment of Love.*" *ELH,* 31 (1964), 139–55.

1565 BROOKE, C. F. Tucker. "The Marlowe Canon." *PMLA,* 37 (1922), 367–417.

1566 BROOKE, C. F. Tucker. "Marlowe's Versification and Style." *SP,* 19 (1922), 186–205.

1567 BROOKE, C. F. Tucker. "The Reputation of Christopher Marlowe." *Transactions of the Connecticut Academy of Arts and Sciences,* 25 (1922), 347–408.

1568 BROOKE, Nicholas. "Marlowe the Dramatist." *Elizabethan Theatre* (Stratford). Pp. 87–105. **See 277.**

1569 BROOKE, Nicholas. "The Moral Tragedy of Doctor Faustus." *Cambridge Journal,* 5 (1952) 662–87.

1570 BROOKS, Charles. "*Tamburlaine* and Attitudes toward Women." *ELH,* 24 (1957), 1–11.

1571 BROWN, Beatrice Daw. "Marlowe, Faustus, and Simon Magus." *PMLA,* 54 (1939), 82–121.

1572 BROWN, John Russell. "Marlowe and the Actors." *TDR,* 8 (1964), 155–73.

1573 BROWN, William J. "Marlowe's Debasement of Bajazet: Foxe's *Actes and Monuments* and *Tamburlaine, Part I.*" *RenQ,* 24 (1971), 38–48.

1574 BURWICK, Frederick. "Marlowe's *Doctor Faustus:* Two Manners, the Argumentative and the Passionate." *Neuphilologische Mitteilungen,* 70 (1969), 121–45.

1575 CAMDEN, Carroll, Jr. "Marlowe and Elizabethan Psychology." *PQ,* 8 (1929), 69–78.

1576 CAMDEN, Carroll, Jr. "Tamburlaine: The Choleric Man." *MLN,* 44 (1929), 430–5.

1577 CAMPBELL, Lily B. "Doctor Faustus: A Case of Conscience." *PMLA,* 67 (1952), 219–39.

1578 CARPENTER, Nan Cooke. "Infinite Riches: A Note on Marlovian Unity." *N&Q,* 196 (1951), 50–2.

1579 CLARK, Eleanor Grace. *The Pembroke Plays: A Study in the Marlowe Canon.* Bryn Mawr, Pa.: Bryn Mawr College, 1928.

1580 CLARK, Eleanor Grace. *Ralegh and Marlowe: A Study in Elizabethan Fustian.* New York: Fordham University Press, 1941.

1581 COCKCROFT, Robert. "Emblematic Irony: Some Possible Significances of Tamburlaine's Chariot." *RMS,* 12 (1968), 33–55.

1582 COLE, Douglas. "Christopher Marlowe, 1564–1964. A Survey." *ShN,* 14 (1964), 44.

1583 COLE, Douglas. "Faust and Anti-Faust in Modern Drama." *DramaS,* 5 (1966), 39–52.

1584 COLE, Douglas. *Suffering and Evil in the Plays of Christopher Marlowe.* Princeton: Princeton University Press, 1962.

1585 COPE, Jackson I. "Marlowe's *Dido* and the Titillating Children." *ELR,* 4 (1974), 315–25.

1586 COX, Gerard H., III. "Marlowe's *Doctor Faustus* and 'Sin Against the Holy Ghost.' " *HLQ,* 36 (1973), 119–37.

1587 CRABTREE, John. "The Comedy in Marlowe's *Dr. Faustus.*" *FurmS,* 9 (1961), 1–9.

1588 CRAIK, T. W. "Faustus' Damnation Reconsidered." *RenD,* n.s. 2 (1969), 189–96.

1589 CUTTS, John P. *The Left Hand of God: A Critical Interpretation of the Plays of Christopher Marlowe.* Haddonfield, N.J.: Haddonfield House, 1973.

1590 CUTTS, John P. "Tamburlaine: 'as Fierce Achilles was.' " *CompD,* 1 (1967), 105–9.

1591 DAICHES, David. "Language and Action in Marlowe's Tamburlaine." *More Literary Essays.* Edinburgh: Oliver & Boyd, 1968. Pp. 42–69.

1592 D'ANDREA, Antonio. "The Aspiring Mind: A Study of the Machiavellian Element in Marlowe's *Tamburlaine.*" *Yearbook of Italian Studies,* 2 (1972), 51–77.

1593 DAVIDSON, Clifford. "Doctor Faustus at Rome." *SEL,* 9 (1969), 231–9.

1594 DAVIDSON, Clifford. "Doctor Faustus of Wittenberg." *SP,* 59 (1962), 514–23.

1595 DEDEYAN, Charles. *Le Thème de Faust dans la littérature européene.* Paris: Lettres Modernes, 1954.

1596 DENT, Robert W. "Marlowe, Spenser, Donne, Shakespeare—and Joseph Wybarne." *RenQ,* (1969), 360–2.

1597 DESSEN, Alan C. "The Elizabethan Stage Jew and Christian Example: Gerontus, Barabas, and Shylock." *MLQ,* 35 (1974), 231–45.

1598 DICK, Hugh. *"Tamburlaine Sources Once More." SP,* 46 (1949), 154–66.

1599 DUTHIE, G. I. "The Dramatic Structure of Marlowe's *Tamburlaine the Great: Parts I and II.*" *ES,* n.s. 1 (1948), 101–26.

1600 DUTHIE, G. I. "Some Observations on Marlowe's *Doctor Faustus.*" *Archiv,* 203 (1966), 81–96.

1601 ECCLES, Mark. *Christopher Marlowe in London.* Cambridge: Harvard University Press, 1934.

1602 EGAN, Robert. "A Muse of Fire: *Henry V* in the Light of *Tamburlaine.*" *MLQ,* 29 (1968), 15–28.

1603 ELIOT, T. S. "Christopher Marlowe." *Selected Essays.* London: Faber & Faber, 1950.

1604 ELLIS-FERMOR, Una M. *Christopher Marlowe.* London: Methuen, 1927.

1605 FANTA, Christopher G. *Marlowe's "Agonists": An Approach to the Ambiguity of his Plays.* Cambridge: Harvard University Press, 1970.

1606 FEASEY, Lynette, and Eveline FEASEY. "Marlowe and the Christian Humanists." *N&Q,* 196 (1951), 266–8.

1607 FEASEY, Lynette, and Eveline FEASEY. "Marlowe and the Commination Service." *N&Q,* 195 (1950), 156–60.

1608 FEASEY, Lynette, and Eveline FEASEY. "Marlowe and the Prophetic Dooms." *N&Q,* 195 (1950), 365–9, 404–7, 419–21.

1609 FIELER, Frank B. *Tamburlaine, Part I, and Its Audience.* Gainesville: University of Florida Press, 1962.

1610 FLOSDORF, J. W. "The 'Odi et Amo' Theme in *The Jew of Malta.*" *N&Q,* n.s. 7 (1960), 10–14.

1611 FRASER, Russell A. "On Christopher Marlowe." *MQR,* 12 (1973), 136–59.

1612 FREEMAN, Arthur. "Marlowe, Kyd, and the Dutch Church Libel." *ELR,* 3 (1973), 44–52.

1613 FREEMAN, Arthur. "A Source for *The Jew of Malta.*" *N&Q,* n.s. 9 (1962), 139–41.

1614 FRENCH, A. L. "The Philosophy of *Dr. Faustus.*" *EIC,* 20 (1970), 123–42.

1615 FRENCH, William W. "Double View in *Dr. Faustus.*" *WVUPP,* 17 (1970), 3–15.

1616 FREY, Leonard H. "Antithetical Balance in the Opening and Close of *Doctor Faustus.*" *MLQ,* 24 (1963), 350–3.

1617 FRICKER, Robert. "The Dramatic Structure of *Edward II.*" *ES,* 34 (1953), 204–17.

1618 FRIEDENREICH, Kenneth. "Directions in *Tamburlaine* Criticism." *Christopher Marlowe's Tamburlaine Parts I and II: Text and Major Criticism.* Pp. 341–53. See **1534.**

1619 FRIEDENREICH, Kenneth. " 'Huge Greatnesse' Overthrown: The Fall of the Empire in Marlowe's Tamburlaine Plays." *ClioW,* 1 (1972), 37–48.

1620 FRIEDMAN, Alan W. "The Shackling of Accidents in Marlowe's *The Jew of Malta.*" *TSLL,* 8 (1966), 155–67.

1621 FRYE, Roland M. "Marlowe's *Doctor Faustus:* The Repudiation of Humanity." *SAQ,* 55 (1956), 322–8.

1622 GALLOWAY, David. "The Ramus Scene in Marlowe's *The Massacre at Paris.*" *N&Q,* 198 (1953), 146–7.

1623 GARDNER, Helen. "Milton's Satan and the Theme of Damnation in Elizabethan Tragedy." *ES,* 1 (1948), 46–66.

1624 GARDNER, Helen. "The Second Part of *Tamburlaine the Great.*" *MLR,* 37 (1942), 18–24.

1625 GIAMATTI, A. Bartlett. "Marlowe: The Arts of Illusion." *YR,* 61 (1972), 530–43.

1626 GLENN, John R. "The Martyrdom of Ramus in Marlowe's *The Massacre at Paris.*" *PLL,* 9 (1973), 365–79.

1627 GODSHALK, William Leigh. *The Marlovian World Picture.* Studies in English Literature, 93. The Hague: Mouton, 1974.

1628 GODSHALK, William Leigh. "Marlowe's *Dido, Queen of Carthage.*" *ELH,* 38 (1971), 1–18.

1629 GOLDFARB, Russell, and Clare GOLDFARB. "The Seven Deadly Sins in *Dr. Faustus.*" *CLAJ,* 13 (1970), 350–63.

1630 GRAY, Austin K. "Some Observations on Christopher Marlowe, Government Agent." *PMLA,* 43 (1928), 682–700.

1631 GREEN, Clarence. "*Doctor Faustus:* Tragedy of Individualism." *Science and Society,* 10 (1946), 275–83.

1632 GREG, W. W. "The Damnation of Faustus." *MLR,* 41 (1946), 97–107.

1633 HARBAGE, Alfred B. "Innocent Barabas." *TDR,* 8 (1964), 47–58.

1634 HARRISON, Thomas P., Jr. "Further Background for *The Jew of Malta* and *The Massacre at Paris.*" *PQ,* 27 (1948), 52–6.

1635 HARRISON, Thomas P., Jr. "Shakespeare and Marlowe's *Dido, Queen of Carthage.*" *UTSE,* 35 (1956), 57–63.

1636 HATTAWAY, Michael. "The Theology of Marlowe's *Doctor Faustus.*" *RenD,* n.s. 3 (1970), 51–78.

1637 HAWKINS, Sherman. "The Education of Faustus." *SEL,* 6 (1966), 193–209.

1638 HEILMAN, Robert B. "The Tragedy of Knowledge: Marlowe's Treatment of Faustus." *QRL*, 2 (1946), 316–32.

1639 HELLER, Otto. *Faust and Faustus: A Study of Goethe's Relation to Marlowe.* St. Louis, Mo.: Washington University Press, 1931.

1640 HENDERSON, Philip. *And Morning in His Eyes: A Book About Christopher Marlowe.* London: Boriswood, 1937.

1641 HENDERSON, Philip. *Christopher Marlowe.* London: Longmans, Green, 1952.

1642 HERRINGTON, H. W. "Christopher Marlowe—Rationalist." *Essays in Memory of Barrett Wendell.* Cambridge: Harvard University Press, 1926. Pp. 121–52.

1643 HILLIER, Richard L. "The Imagery of Color, Light, and Darkness in the Poetry of Christopher Marlowe." *Elizabethan Studies and Other Essays: In Honor of George F. Reynolds.* Boulder: University of Colorado Press, 1945. Pp. 101–25.

1644 HOMAN, Sidney R., Jr. "Chapman and Marlowe: The Paradoxical Hero and the Divided Response." *JEGP,* 68 (1969), 391–406.

1645 HONDERICH, Pauline. "John Calvin and *Doctor Faustus.*" *MLR,* 68 (1973), 1–13.

1646 HOTSON, Leslie. *The Death of Christopher Marlowe.* London: Nonesuch Press, 1925.

1647 HOUK, Raymond. "*Doctor Faustus* and *A Shrew.*" *PMLA,* 62 (1947), 950–7.

1648 HOY, Cyrus. " 'Ignorance in Knowledge': Marlowe's Faustus and Ford's Giovanni." *MP,* 57 (1960), 145–54.

1649 HSIN, Fang. "*Macbeth* as a Morality Play: A Comparative Study of the Play with Reference to *Everyman* and *Doctor Faustus.*" *Fu Jen Studies,* 7 (1974), 1–24.

1650 HUNTER, G. K. "Five-Act Structure in *Doctor Faustus.*" *TDR,* 8 (1964), 77–91.

1651 HUNTER, G. K. "The Theology of Marlowe's *The Jew of Malta.*" *JWCI,* 27 (1964), 211–40.

1652 IZARD, Thomas C. "The Principal Source for Marlowe's *Tamburlaine.*" *MLN,* 58 (1943), 411–7.

1653 JACQUOT, Jean. "La Pensée de Marlowe dans *Tamburlaine the Great.*" *EA,* 6 (1953), 322–45.

1654 JANZ, Harold. "An Elizabethan Statement on the Origin of the German Faust Book. With a Note on Marlowe's Sources." *JEGP,* 51 (1952), 137–53.

1655 JENSEN, Ejner. "Marlowe Our Contemporary?" *CE,* 30 (1969), 627–32.

1656 JOHNSON, Francis R. "Marlowe's Astronomy and Renaissance Skepticism." *ELH,* 13 (1946), 241–54.

1657 JOHNSON, Francis R. "Marlowe's 'Imperial Heaven.' " *EHL,* 12 (1945), 35–44.

1658 JOHNSON, S. F. "Marlowe's *Edward II.*" *Explicator,* 10 (1952), 53.

1659 KAHLER, Erich. "Doctor Faustus from Adam to Sartre." *CompD,* 1 (1967), 75–92.

1660 KAULA, David. "Time and the Timeless in *Everyman* and *Doctor Faustus.*" *CE,* 22 (1960), 9–14.

1661 KIESSLING, Nicolas. "Doctor Faustus and the Sin of Demoniality." *SEL,* 15 (1975), 205–11.

1662 KIMBROUGH, Robert. "*Tamburlaine: A Speaking Picture in a Tragic Glass.*" *RenD.* 7 (1964), 20–34.

1663 KIRSCHBAUM, Leo. "Marlowe's *Faustus:* A Reconsideration." *RES,* 19 (1943), 225–41.

1664 KIRSCHBAUM, Leo. "Some Light on *The Jew of Malta.*" *MLQ,* 7 (1946), 53–6.

1665 KNOLL, Robert E. *Christopher Marlowe.* New York: Twayne, 1969.

1666 KOCHER, Paul H. "Backgrounds for Marlowe's Atheist Lecture." *Renaissance Studies in Honor of Hardin Craig.* Stanford: Stanford University Press, 1941. Pp. 112–32. [Also in *PQ,* 20 (1942), 304–24.]

1667 KOCHER, Paul H. *Christopher Marlowe: A Study of His Thought, Learning and Character.* Chapel Hill: University of North Carolina Press, 1946.

1668 KOCHER, Paul H. "Christopher Marlowe, Individualist." *UTQ,* 17 (1948), 111–20.

1669 KOCHER, Paul H. "Contemporary Pamphlet Backgrounds for Marlowe's *The Massacre at Paris.*" *MLQ,* 8 (1947), 151–73, 309–18.

1670 KOCHER, Paul H. "The Development of Marlowe's Character." *PQ,* 17 (1938), 331–50.

1671 KOCHER, Paul H. "English Legal History in Marlowe's *Jew of Malta.*" *HLQ* 26 (1963), 155–63.

1672 KOCHER, Paul H. "François Hotman and Marlowe's *The Massacre at Paris.*" *PMLA,* 56 (1941), 349–68.

1673 KOCHER, Paul H. "A Marlowe Sonnet." *PQ,* 24 (1945), 39–45.

1674 KOCHER, Paul H. "Marlowe's Art of War." *SP,* 39 (1942), 207–25.

1675 KOCHER, Paul H. "Marlowe's Atheist Lecture." *JEGP,* 39 (1940), 98–106.

1676 KOCHER, Paul H. "Nashe's Authorship of the Prose Scenes in *Faustus.*" *MLQ,* 3 (1942), 17–40.

1677 KOCHER, Paul H. "The Witchcraft Basis in Marlowe's *Faustus.*" *MP,* 38 (1940) 9–36.

1678 KURIYAMA, Constance Brown. "Dr. Greg and *Doctor Faustus:* The Supposed Originality of the 1616 Text." *ELR,* 5 (1975), 171–97.

1679 KURUKAWA, Takashi. "*De Casibus* Theme and Machiavellism—In Connection with the Theme of *Edward II.*" *SS,* 7 (1968–69), 61–80.

1680 LANGSTON, Beach. "Marlowe's *Faustus* and the *Ars Moriendi* Tradition." *A Tribute to George Coffin Taylor.* Chapel Hill: University of North Carolina Press, 1952. Pp. 148–67.

1681 LAWRENCE, C. E. "Christopher Marlowe, the Man." *Quarterly Review,* 255 (1930), 231–46.

1682 LEECH, Clifford, ed. *Marlowe: A Collection of Critical Essays.* Englewood Cliffs, N.J.: Prentice-Hall, 1965.

1683 LEECH, Clifford. "Marlowe's *Edward II:* Power and Suffering." *Critical Quarterly,* 1 (1959), 181–96.

1684 LEECH, Clifford. "Marlowe's Humor." *Essays on Shakespeare and Elizabethan Drama.* Pp. 69–82. **See 287.**

1685 LEECH, Clifford. "The Structure of *Tamburlaine.*" *TDR,* 8 (1964), 32–46.

1686 LEPAGE, Peter V. "The Search for Godhead in Marlowe's *Tamburlaine.*" *CE* 26, (1965), 604–9.

1687 LESLIE, Nancy T. "*Tamburlaine in the Theater: Tartar, Grand Guignol, or Janus?*" *RenD,* (1971), 105–20.

1688 LEVER, Katherine. "The Image of Man in *Tamburlaine, Part I.*" *PQ,* 35 (1956), 421–7.

1689 LEVIN, Harry. "Marlowe Today." *TDR,* 8 (1964), 22–31.

1690 LEVIN, Harry. *The Overreacher: A Study of Christopher Marlowe.* Cambridge: Harvard University Press, 1952.

1691 LONGO, Joseph A. "Marlowe's *Doctor Faustus:* Allegorical Parody in Act Five." *Greyfriar,* 15 (1974), 38–49.

1692 McALINDON, T. "Classical Mythology and Christian Tradition in Marlowe's *Doctor Faustus.*" *PMLA,* 71 (1966), 214–23.

1693 McCLOSKEY, John C. "The Theme of Despair in Marlowe's *Faustus.*" *CE,* 4 (1942), 110–3.

1694 McCULLEN, Joseph T., Jr. "Dr. Faustus and Renaissance Learning." *MLR,* 51 (1956), 6–16.

1695 MAHOOD, M. M. *Poetry and Humanism.* New Haven: Yale University Press, 1950. Pp. 54–86.

1696 MANLEY, Frank. "The Nature of Faustus." *MP,* 66 (1969), 218–31.

1697 MASINTON, Charles G. *Christopher Marlowe's Tragic Vision: A Study in Damnation.* Athens: Ohio University Press, 1972.

1698 MASINTON, Charles G. "Marlowe's Artists: The Failure of Imagination." *Ohio State University Review,* 11 (1969), 22–35.

1699 MATALENE, H. W., III. "Marlowe's *Faustus* and the Comforts of Academicism." *ELH,* 39 (1972), 495–520.

1700 MAXWELL, J. C. "How Bad is the Text of *The Jew of Malta?*" *MLR,* 48 (1953), 435–8.

1701 MAXWELL, J. C. "The Plays of Christopher Marlowe." *The Age of Shakespeare.* Pelican Guide to English Literature 2, Boris Ford, ed. Baltimore: Penguin, 1955. Pp. 162–78.

1702 MEEHAN, Virginia Mary. *Christopher Marlowe: Poet and Playwright. Studies in Poetical Method.* The Hague: Mouton, 1974.

1703 MIZENER, Arthur. "The Tragedy of Marlowe's *Doctor Faustus. CE,* 5 (1943), 70–5.

1704 MORGAN, Gerald. "Harlequin Faustus: Marlowe's Comedy of Hell." *HAB,* 18 (1967), 22–34.

1705 MORRIS, B., ed. *Christopher Marlowe.* Mermaid Critical Commentaries. New York: Hill & Wang, 1969.

1706 MORRIS, Harry. "Marlowe's [Dramatic] Poetry." *TDR,* 8 (1964) 134–54.

1707 NELSON, Timothy G. A. "Marlowe and His Audience: A Study of *Tamburlaine.*" *SoRA,* 3 (1969), 249–63.

1708 NOGARAJAN, S. "The Philosophy of *Dr. Faustus.*" *EIC,* 20 (1970), 123–42.

1709 NORMAN, C. *The Muses' Darling: The Life of Christopher Marlowe*. New York: Rinehart, 1946.

1710 NOZAKI, Mutsumi. "The Comic Sense in Marlowe Reconsidered." *ShStud*, 9 (1970–71), 1–27.

1711 O'BRIEN, Margaret Ann. "Christian Belief in *Dr. Faustus.*" *ELH*, 37 (1970), 1–11.

1712 O'NEILL, Judith, ed. *Critics on Marlowe*. Coral Gables, Fla.: University of Miami Press, 1970.

1713 ORNSTEIN, Robert. "The Comic Synthesis in *Doctor Faustus.*" *ELH*, 22 (1955), 165–72.

1714 ORNSTEIN, Robert. "Marlowe and God: The Tragic Theology of *Dr. Faustus.*" *PMLA*, 83 (1968), 1378–85.

1715 PALMER, D. J. "Magic and Poetry in *Doctor Faustus.*" *CR*, 6 (1964) 56–7.

1716 PARFITT, G. A. E. "Some Notes on the Classical Borrowings in *Volpone.*" *ES*, 55 (1974), 127–32.

1717 PARR, Johnstone. *Tamburlaine's Malady and Other Essays on Astrology in Elizabethan Drama*. Tuscaloosa: University of Alabama Press, 1953.

1718 PEARCE, T. M. "Marlowe and Castiglione." *MLQ*, 12 (1951), 3–12.

1719 PEARCE, T. M. "Tamburlaine's 'Discipline to His Three Sonnes': An Interpretation of *Tamburlaine, Part II.*" *MLQ*, 15 (1945), 18–27.

1720 PEAVY, Charles E. "*The Jew of Malta*—Anti-Semitic or Anti-Catholic?" *McNeese Review*, 11 (1959), 57–61.

1721 PEERY, William. "Marlowe's Irreverent Humor—Some Open Questions." *Tulane Studies in English*, 6 (1956), 15–29.

1722 PEET, Donald. "The Rhetoric of *Tamburlaine.*" *ELH*, 26 (1959), 137–55.

1723 PERRET, Marion. "*Edward II:* Marlowe's Dramatic Technique." *REL*, 7 (1966), 87–91.

1724 PESCHMANN, Hermann. "Christopher Marlowe, 1564–1593: 'Infinite Riches in a Little Room.' " *English*, 15 (1969), 85–9.

1725 PHELPS, William Lyon. "Marlowe." *Essays on Books*. New York: Macmillan, 1922.

1726 POIRIER, Michel. *Christopher Marlowe*. London: Chatto & Windus, 1951.

1727 POWELL, Jocelyn. "Marlowe's Spectacle." *TDR*, 8 (1964), 195–210.

1728 PRAZ, Mario. "Il Dotter Fausto: Marlowe e Goethe." *La Cultura*, 11 (1932), 238–47.

1729 QUINN, Michael. "The Freedom of Tamburlaine." *MLQ*, 21 (1960), 315–20.

1730 REYNOLDS, James A. "Marlowe's *Dr. Faustus:* 'Be a Divine in Show' and 'When All Is Done, Divinity Is Best'." *American Notes and Queries*, 13 (1975), 131–3.

1731 RIBNER, Irving. "The Idea of History in Marlowe's *Tamburlaine.*" *ELH*, 20 (1954), 251–66.

1732 RIBNER, Irving. "Marlowe and Machiavelli." *CL*, 6 (1954), 348–56.

1733 RIBNER, Irving. "Marlowe and Shakespeare." *SQ*, 15 (1964), 41–53.

1734 RIBNER, Irving. "Marlowe and the Critics." *TDR*, 8 (1964), 211–25.

1735 RIBNER, Irving. "Marlowe's *Edward II* and the Tudor History Play." *ELH.* 22 (1955), 243–53.

1736 RIBNER, Irving. "Marlowe's 'Tragicke Glasse.'" *Essays on Shakespeare and Elizabethan Drama.* Pp. 91–114. **See 287.**

1737 RIBNER, Irving. "*Tamburlaine* and *The Wars of Cyrus.*" *JEGP.* 53 (1954), 564–73.

1738 RICHARDS, Susan. "Marlowe's *Tamburlaine II:* A Drama of Death." *MLQ.* 26 (1965), 375–87.

1739 RICHMOND, Velma Bourgeois. "Renaissance Sexuality and Marlowe's Women." *BSUF,* 16, iv(1975), 36–44.

1740 RICKY, Mary Ellen. "Astronomical Imagery in *Tamburlaine.*" *RenP 1954,* (1955) 463–70.

1741 ROBERTSON, J. M. *Marlowe: A Conspectus.* London: Routledge, 1931.

1742 ROBERTSON, Toby. "Directing *Edward II.*" *TDR.* 8 (1964), 174–83.

1743 ROGERS, David M. "Love and Honor in Marlowe's *Dido, Queen of Carthage.*" *Grayfriar,* 6 (1963), 3–7.

1744 RÖHRMAN, H. *Marlowe and Shakespeare: A Thematic Exposition of Their Plays.* Arnhem: Van Loghum Slaterus, 1952.

1745 ROSS, W. H. *Kind Kit: An Informal Biography of Christopher Marlowe.* New York: St. Martin's, 1973.

1746 ROTHSTEIN, Eric. "Structure as Meaning in *The Jew of Malta.*" *JEGP.* 65 (1966), 260–73.

1747 ROWSE, A. L. *Christopher Marlowe: His Life and Work.* New York: Harper & Row, 1964.

1748 SACHS, Arieh. "The Religious Despair of Doctor Faustus." *JEGP.* 63 (1964), 625–47.

1749 SANDERS, Wilbur. *The Dramatist and the Received Idea: Studies in the Plays of Marlowe and Shakespeare.* Cambridge: Cambridge University Press, 1968.

1750 SCHUSTER, Erika, and Horst OPPEL. "Die Bankett-Szene in Marlowes *Tamburlaine.*" *Anglia,* 77 (1959), 310–45.

1751 SEATON, Ethel. "Fresh Sources for Marlowe." *RES.* 5 (1929), 385–401.

1752 SEATON, Ethel. "Marlowe's Light Reading." *Elizabethan and Jacobean Studies.* Pp. 17–35. **See 280.**

1753 SEATON, Ethel. "Marlowe's Map." *E&S 1924,* (1925), 13–35.

1754 SEGAL, Erich. "Marlowe's Schadenfreude: Barabas as Comic Hero." In *Veins of Humor.* Cambridge: Harvard University Press, 1972. Pp. 69–91.

1755 SELLIN, Paul R. "The Hidden God: Reformation Awe in Renaissance Literature." *The Darker Vision of the Renaissance: Beyond the Fields of Reason.* Berkeley: University of California Press, 1974. Pp. 147–96.

1756 SIMMONS, J. L. "Elizabethan Stage Practice and Marlowe's *The Jew of Malta.*" *RenD,* 4 (1971), 93–104.

1757 SIMPSON, Percy. "Marlowe's *Tragical History of Dr. Faustus.*" *ES.* 14 (1929), 20–34.

1758 SMITH, Hallett. "*Tamburlaine* and the Renaissance." *Elizabethan Studies and Other Essays: In Honor of George F. Reynolds.* Boulder: University of Colorado Press, 1945. Pp. 126–31.

1759 SMITH, James. "Marlowe's *Dr. Faustus.*" *Scrutiny,* 8 (1939), 36–55.

1760 SMITH, Marion B. *Marlowe's Imagery and the Marlowe Canon.* Philadelphia: University of Pennsylvania Press, 1940.

1761 SMITH, Marion B. "The Substance of Meaning in *Tamburlaine Part I.*" *SP,* 67 (1970), 156–66.

1762 SMITH, Warren D. "The Nature of Evil in *Doctor Faustus.*" *MLR,* 60 (1965), 171–5.

1763 SNYDER, Susan. "Marlowe's *Dr. Faustus* as an Inverted Saint's Life." *SP,* 63 (1966), 565–77.

1764 SPEAIGHT, Robert. "Marlowe: The Forerunner." *REL,* 7 (1966), 25–41.

1765 SPENCE, Leslie. "Tamburlaine and Marlowe." *PMLA,* 42 (1927), 604–22.

1766 STEANE, J. B. *Marlowe: A Critical Study.* Cambridge: Cambridge University Press, 1964.

1767 STROUP, Thomas B. "*Doctor Faustus* and *Hamlet:* Contrasting Kinds of Christian Tragedy." *CompD,* 5 (1971–72), 243–53.

1768 STROUP, Thomas B. "Ritual in Marlowe's Plays." *CompD,* 7 (1973), 198–221.

1769 SUMMERS, Claude J. "Tamburlaine's Opponents and Machiavelli's *Prince.*" *ELN,* 11 (1974), 256–8.

1770 SUNESEN, Bent. "Marlowe and the Dumb Show." *ES,* 35 (1954), 241–53.

1771 SYLER, Siegfried. "Marlowe's Technique of Communicating with His Audience, as Seen in His *Tamburlaine, Part I.*" *ES,* 48 (1967), 306–16.

1772 SYMONS, Arthur. "A Note on the Genius of Marlowe." *English Review,* 36 (1923), 306–16.

1773 TAYLOR, George Coffin. "Marlowe's 'Now.'" *Elizabethan Studies and Other Essays: In Honor of George F. Reynolds.* Boulder: University of Colorado Press, 1945. Pp. 93–125.

1774 TAYLOR, Rupert. "A Tentative Chronology of Marlowe's and Some Other Elizabethan Plays." *PMLA,* 51 (1936), 643–88.

1775 THIMME, Margaret. "Marlowe's 'Jew of Malta.' Stil- und Echtheitsfragen." *Studien zur englischen Philologie.* Halle: M. Niemeyer, 1921.

1776 THORP, Willard. "The Ethical Problem in Marlowe's *Tamburlaine.*" *JEGP,* 29 (1930), 385–9.

1777 TIBI, Pierre. "*Dr. Faustus* et la cosmologie de Marlowe." *RLV,* 40 (1974), 212–27.

1778 TILLEY, Morris P., and James K. ROY. "Proverbs and Proverbial Allusions in Marlowe." *MLN,* 50 (1935), 347–55.

1779 TRACI, J. "Marlowe's Faustus as Artist: A Suggestion About a Theme in the Play." *RenP 1966,* (1967), 3–9.

1780 TURNER, Robert Y. "Shakespeare and the Public Confrontation Scene in Early History Plays." *MP,* 62 (1964), 1–12.

1781 VERSFELD, Martin. "Some Remarks on Marlowe's *Faustus.*" *ESA,* 1 (1958), 134–43.

1782 WAITH, Eugene M. "*Edward II:* The Shadow of Action." *TDR,* 8 (1964), 59–76.

1783 WAITH, Eugene M. *The Herculean Hero in Marlowe, Chapman, Shakespeare and Dryden.* New York: Columbia University Press, 1962.

1784 WAITH, Eugene M. "Marlowe and the Jades of Asia." *SEL,* 5 (1965), 229–45.

1785 WALSH, Maureen P. "Demigod, Devil, or Man: A Reconsideration of the Character of Faustus." *Nassau Review* (Nassau [N.Y.] Comm. Coll.), 2 (1970), 54–65.

1786 WASWO, Richard. "Damnation, Protestant Style: Macbeth, Faustus, and Christian Tragedy." *JMRS,* 4 (1974), 64–99.

1787 WATSON-WILLIAMS, Helen. "The Power of Words: A Reading of *Tamburlaine the Great, Part One.*" *English,* 22 (1973), 13–18.

1788 WEST, Robert H. "The Impatient Magic of *Dr. Faustus.*" *ELR,* 4 (1974), 218–40.

1789 WESTLUND, Joseph. "The Orthodox Christian Framework of Marlowe's *Faustus.*" *SEL,* 3 (1963), 191–205.

1790 WICKHAM, Glynne. "*Exeunt to the Cave:* Notes on the Staging of Marlowe's Plays." *TDR,* 8 (1964), 184–94.

1791 WILSON, F. P. *Marlowe and the Early Shakespeare.* Oxford: The Clarendon Press, 1953.

1792 WYLER, Siegrfied. "Marlowe's Technique of Communication with His Audience, as Seen in His *Tamburlaine Part I.*" *ES,* 48 (1967), 306–16.

1793 WYMAN, Linda. "How Plot and Sub-Plot Unite in Marlowe's *Faustus.*" *CEA Critic,* 37, i(1974), 14–6.

1794 ZANCO, Aurelio. "La Biografia di Christopher Marlowe alla luce degli studi moderni." *Annali della facoltà di lettere della R. Università di Cagliari* (1933–35), 155–82.

1795 ZANCO, Aurelio. *Christopher Marlowe: Saggio critico.* Firenze: La Nuova Italia, 1937.

1796 ZIMANSKY, Curt A. "Marlowe's *Faustus:* The Date Again." *PQ,* 41 (1962), 181–7.

Marston, John (1575?–1634)

Bibliography

1797 PENNEL, and WILLIAMS, eds. See 830.

Works

1798 *The Works of John Marston.* 3 vols. A. H. Bullen, ed. London: Nimmo, 1887.

1799 *The Works of John Marston.* 3 vols. H. Harvey Wood, ed. Edinburgh: Oliver & Boyd, 1934–8.

1800 *Antonio and Mellida: The First Part.* G. K. Hunter, ed. Regents Renaissance Drama Series. Lincoln: University of Nebraska Press, 1965.

1801 *Antonio's Revenge: The Second Part of Antonio and Mellida.* G. K. Hunter, ed. Regents Renaissance Drama Series. Lincoln: University of Nebraska Press, 1965.

1802 *The Dutch Courtesan.* Peter Davidson, ed. Fountainwell. Berkeley: University of California Press, 1968.

1803 *The Dutch Courtesan.* M. L. Wine, ed. Regents Renaissance Drama Series. Lincoln: University of Nebraska Press, 1965.

1804 *The Fawn.* Gerald A. Smith, ed. Regents Renaissance Drama Series. Lincoln: University of Nebraska Press, 1965.

1805 *The Malcontent.* Bernard Harris, ed. New Mermaids. New York: Hill & Wang, 1967.

1806 *The Malcontent.* G. K. Hunter, ed. London: Methuen, 1975.

1807 *The Malcontent.* M. L. Wine, ed. Regents Renaissance Drama Series. Lincoln: University of Nebraska Press, 1964.

Studies

1808 AGGELER, Geoffrey. "Stoicism and Revenge in Marston." *ES,* 51 (1971), 507–17.

1809 ALLEN, Morse S. *The Satire of John Marston.* Columbus: Ohio State University Press, 1920.

1810 ANDREWS, Michael C. "*Jack Drum's Entertainment* as Burlesque." *RenQ,* 24 (1971), 226–31.

1811 [ANON.] "Theatre of Cruelty in the Middle Temple." *TLS,* (5 Feb 1971), 155–7.

1812 AXELRAD, A. José. *Un Malcontent Elizabéthain: John Marston (1576–1634).* Paris: Didier, 1955.

1813 AXELRAD, A. José. "Sur une Source possible de la *Sophonisbe* de John Marston (1606)." *RLC,* 27 (1953), 182–6.

1814 AYRES, Philip J. "Marston's *Antonio's Revenge:* The Morality of the Revenging Hero." *SEL,* 12 (1972), 359–74.

1815 BERGSON, Allen. "Dramatic Style as Parody in Marston's *Antonio and Mellida.*" *SEL,* 11 (1971), 307–25.

1816 BERGSON, Allen. "The Ironic Tragedies of Marston and Chapman: Notes on Jacobean Tragic Form." *JEGP,* 69 (1970), 613–30.

1817 BERLAND, Ellen. "The Function of Irony in Marston's *Antonio and Mellida.*" *SP,* 66 (1969), 739–55.

1818 BRETTLE, R. E. "John Marston, Dramatist, at Oxford, 1591(?)–1594, 1609." *RES,* 3 (1927), 398–405.

1819 BRETTLE, R. E. "John Marston, Dramatist: Some New Facts About His Life." *MLR,* 22 (1927), 7–14, 17.

1820 BRETTLE, R. E. "More Bibliographical Notes on Marston." *The Library,* N.S. 12 (1931), 235–42.

1821 BRETTLE, R. E. "Notes on John Marston." *RES,* n.s. 13 (1962), 390–93.

1822 CAPUTI, Anthony. *John Marston, Satirist.* Ithaca, N.Y.: Cornell University Press, 1961.

1823 COHEN, Ralph A. "The Function of Setting in *Eastward Ho.*" *RenP 1973*, (1974), 83–96.

1824 COLLEY, John Scott. *John Marston's Theatrical Drama.* Jacobean Drama Studies 33. Salzburg: Institut für Englische Sprache und Literatur, Univerität Salzburg, 1974.

1825 CROSS, Gustav. "The Date of *The Malcontent* Once More." *PQ,* 39 (1960), 104–13.

1826 CROSS, Gustav. "Marston, Montaigne and Morality: *The Dutch Courtezan* Reconsidered." *ELH,* 27 (1960), 30–43.

1827 CROSS, Gustav. "The Retrograde Genius of John Marston." *REL,* 2 (1961), 19–27.

1828 CROSS, Gustav. "Some Notes on the Vocabulary of John Marston." *N&Q,* 199 (1954), 425–7; 200 (1955), 20–1, 57–8, 186–7, 335–6, 427–9, 480–2; 201 (1956), 331–2, 470–1; 202 (1957), 65–6, 221–3, 283–5, 524–6; 203 (1958), 5–6, 103–4, 221–2; 204 (1959), 101–2, 137–9, 254–5, 355–6; 205 (1960), 135–6; 206 (1961), 123–6, 298–300, 388–91; 208 (1963), 308–12.

1829 FABER, J. Arthur. "Rhetorical Strategy in John Marston's *The Malcontent. HussR,* 4 (1970), 18–24.

1830 FINKELPEARL, Philip J. *John Marston of the Middle Temple.* Cambridge: Harvard University Press, 1969.

1831 FOAKES, R. A. "John Marston's Fantastical Plays: *Antonio and Mellida* and *Antonio's Revenge.*" *PQ,* 41 (1962), 229–39.

1832 GECKLE, George L. "*Antonio's Revenge:* 'Never More Woe in Lesser Plot was Found.'" *CompD,* 6 (1972–73), 323–35.

1833 GECKLE, George L. "Fortune in Marston's *The Malcontent.*" *PMLA,* 86 (1971), 202–9.

1834 GECKLE, George L. "John Marston's *Histriomastix* and the Golden Age." *CompD,* 6 (1972–3), 205–22.

1835 GIBBONS, Brian. See **642.**

1836 GILL, Roma. "A Purchase of Glory: The Persona of Late Elizabethan Satire." *SP,* 72 (1975), 408–18.

1837 GREENMAN, David J. "Atmosphere, Contrast, and Control in Marston's *The Malcontent.*" *Shakespeare Jahrbuch (Weimar),* (1975), 134–44.

1838 HAMILTON, Donna B. "Language as Theme in *The Dutch Courtesan.*" *RenD,* n.s. 5 (1972), 75–88.

1839 HIGGINS, Michael. "The Convention of the Stoic Hero as Handled by Marston." *MLR,* 39 (1944), 338–46.

1840 HIRST, Désirée. "The Enigmatic Mr. Marston." *AntigR,* 1 (1970), 97–9.

1841 HOUSER, David J. "Purging the Commonwealth: Marston's Disguised Dukes and *A Knack to Know a Knave.*" *PMLA,* 89 (1974), 993–1006.

1842 HUNTER, G. K. "English Folly and Italian Vice: The Moral Landscape of John Marston." *Jacobean Theatre.* Pp. 85–112. See **276.**

1843 JACKSON, James L. "Sources of the Sub-Plot of Marston's *The Dutch Courtezan.*" *PQ,* 31 (1952), 223–4.

1844 JENSEN, Ejner. "Theme and Imagery in *The Malcontent.*" *SEL*, 10 (1970), 367–84.

1845 KAPLAN, Joel H. "John Marston's *Fawn:* A Saturnalian Satire." *SEL*, 9 (1969), 335–50.

1846 KERNAN, Alvin. "John Marston's Play *Histriomastix.*" *MLQ*, 19 (1958), 134–40.

1847 KIEFER, Christian. "Music and Marston's *The Malcontent. SP*, 51 (1954), 163–71.

1848 LOCKERT, Lacy. "Marston, Webster, and the Decline of the Elizabethan Drama." *SR*, 27 (1919), 62–81.

1849 McGINN, Donald J. "A New Date for *Antonio's Revenge.*" *PMLA*, 53 (1938), 129–37.

1850 O'CONNOR, John J. "The Chief Source of Marston's *Dutch Courtezan.*" *SP*, 54 (1957), 509–15.

1851 O'NEILL, David G. "The Commencement of Marston's Career as a Dramatist." *RES*, 22 (1971), 442–5.

1852 ORRELL, John. "The Sources of Marston's *The Wonder of Women or The Tragedie of Sophonisba.*" *N&Q*, n.s. 10 (1963), 102–3.

1853 PELLEGRINI, Giuliano. *Il Teatro di John Marston.* Pisa: Libraria Goliardica Editrice, 1952.

1854 PETER, John. "John Marston's Plays." *Scrutiny*, 17 (1950), 132–53.

1855 PETER, John. "Marston's Use of Seneca." *N&Q*, 199 (1954), 145–9.

1856 PRESSON, Robert K. "Marston's *Dutch Courtezan:* The Study of an Attitude in Adaptation." *JEGP*, 55 (1956), 406–13.

1857 SALOMON, Brownell. "The Theological Basis of Imagery and Structure in *The Malcontent.*" *SEL*, 14 (1974), 271–84.

1858 SCHOENBAUM, S. "The Precarious Balance of John Marston." *PMLA*, 67 (1952), 1069–78.

1859 SIEMON, James Edward. "Disguise in Marston and Shakespeare." *HLQ*, 38 (1975), 105–23.

1860 SLIGHTS, William W. E. " 'Elder in a Deformed Church': The Function of Marston's Malcontent." *SEL*, 13 (1973), 360–73.

1861 SLIGHTS, William W. E. "Political Morality and the Ending of *The Malcontent.*" *MP*, 69 (1971), 138–9.

1862 SPENCER, Theodore. "Reason and Passion in Marston's *The Dutch Courtezan.*" *Criterion*, 13 (1934), 586–94.

1863 STAGG, Louis C. *An Index to the Figurative Language of John Marston's Tragedies.* Charlottesville: Bibliographical Society of the University of Virginia, 1970.

1864 STOLL, E. E. "The Date of *The Malcontent:* A Rejoinder." *RES*, 11 (1935), 42–50.

1865 STOLL, E. E. "Shakspere, Marston, and the Malcontent Type." *MP*, 3 (1906), 281–303.

1866 UPTON, Albert W. "Allusions to James I and His Court in Marston's *Fawn* and Beaumont's *Woman Hater.*" *PMLA*, 44 (1929), 1048–65.

1867 URE, Peter. John Marston's *Sophonisba:* A Reconsideration." *DUJ,* 10 (1949), 81–90.

1868 WALLEY, Harold R. "The Dates of *Hamlet* and Marston's *Malcontent."* *RES,* 9 (1933), 397–409.

1869 WEST, Robert H. "The Impatient Magic of *Dr. Faustus."* *ELR,* 4 (1974), 218–40.

1870 WHARTON, T. F. "*The Malcontent* and 'Dreams, Visions, Fantasies.' " *EIC,* 24 (1974), 261–73.

1871 WHARTON, T. F. "Old Marston or New Marston: The *Antonio* Plays." *EIC,* 25 (1975), 357–69.

1872 ZALL, Paul M. "John Marston, Moralist." *ELH,* 20 (1953), 186–93.

Massinger, Philip (1583–1640)

Bibliography

1873 PENNEL, and WILLIAMS, eds. See **748.**

Works

1874 *The Plays of Philip Massinger.* 4 vols. F. Cunningham, ed. London: Hotten, 1871.

1875 *The City Madam.* Cyrus Hoy, ed. Regents Renaissance Drama Series. Lincoln: University of Nebraska Press, 1964.

1876 *The Fatal Dowry.* T. A. Dunn, ed. Fountainwell. Berkeley: University of California Press, 1969.

1877 *A New Way to Pay Old Debts.* M. St. C. Byrne, ed. London: Athlone Press, 1956.

Studies

1878 BALL, Robert H. *The Amazing Career of Sir Giles Overreach.* Princeton: Princeton University Press, 1939.

1879 BENNETT, A. L. "The Moral Tone of Massinger's Dramas." *PLL,* 2 (1966), 207–16.

1880 BURELBACH, Frederick, "*A New Way to Pay Old Debts:* Jacobean Morality." *CLAJ,* 12 (1969), 205–13.

1881 CHELLI, M. *Le Drame de Massinger.* Paris: Société d'Éditions "Les Belles Lettres," 1924.

1882 CHELLI, M. *Etude sur la collaboration de Massinger avec Fletcher et son groupe.* Paris: Presses universitaires, 1926.

1883 CLUBB, Louise George. "*The Virgin Martyr* and the *Tragedia Sacra."* *RenD,* 7 (1964), 103–26.

1884 CRUICKSHANK, A. H. *Philip Massinger.* Oxford: Basil Blackwell, 1920.

1885 DAVISON, Peter. "The Theme and Structure of *The Roman Actor."* *Journal of the Australian Universities Language and Literature Association,* 19 (1963), 39–56.

1886 DUNN, T. A. *Philip Massinger: The Man and the Playwright.* Edinburgh: Thomas Nelson & Sons, 1957.

1887 EDWARDS, Philip. "Massinger the Censor." *Essays on Shakespeare and Elizabethan Drama.* Pp. 341–50. **See 287.**

1888 EDWARDS, Philip. "The Royal Pretenders in Massinger and Ford." *E&S 1974,* 18–36.

1889 EDWARDS, Philip. "The Sources of Massinger's *The Bondman.*" *RES,* 15 (1964), 21–6.

1890 ENRIGHT, D. J. "Poetic Satire and Satire in Verse: A Consideration of Jonson and Massinger." *Scrutiny,* 18 (1951–52), 211–23.

1891 EVENHUIS, Francis D. *Massinger's Imagery.* Jacobean Drama Studies 14. Salzburg: Institut Für Englische Sprache und Literatur, Universität Salzburg, 1973.

1892 FOTHERGILL, Robert A. "The Dramatic Experience of Massinger's *The City Madam* and *A New Way to Pay Old Debts.*" *UTQ,* 43 (1973), 68–86.

1893 GARDINER, S. R. "The Political Element in Massinger." *Contemporary Review,* 38 (1876), 315–31.

1894 GARROD, H. W. "Massinger." *The Profession of Poetry.* Oxford: The Clarendon Press, 1929. Pp. 225–39.

1895 GIBSON, C. A. "Massinger's London Merchant and the Date of the *City Madam.*" *MLR,* 65 (1970), 737–49.

1896 GILL, Roma. "Collaboration and Revision in Massinger's *A Very Woman.*" *RES,* 18 (1967), 136–48.

1897 GROSS, Allen. "Contemporary Politics in Massinger." *SEL,* 6 (1966), 279–90.

1898 GROSS, Allen. "Social Change and Philip Massinger." *SEL,* 7 (1967), 329–42.

1899 HOGAN, A. P. "Imagery of Acting in *The Roman Actor.*" *MLR,* 66 (1971), 273–81.

1900 HOY, Cyrus. "Verbal Formulae in the Plays of Philip Massinger." *SP,* 56 (1959), 600–18.

1901 JONES, Frederic L. "An Experiment with Massinger's Verse." *PMLA,* 47 (1932), 727–40.

1902 LAWLESS, Donald S. *Philip Massinger and His Associates.* Ball State Monograph 10. Indianapolis, Ind.: Ball State University Press, 1967.

1903 LYONS, John O. "Massinger's Imagery." *Ren P 1955,* (1956), 47–54.

1904 McILWRAITH, A. K. "The Manuscript Corrections in Massinger's Plays." *The Library,* 6 (1952), 213–6.

1905 McILWRAITH, A. K. "Some Bibliographical Notes on Massinger." *The Library,* n.s. 11 (1930), 78–92.

1906 MAKKINK, H. J. *Philip Massinger and John Fletcher: A Comparison.* Rotterdam: Nijgh & Van Ditmar, 1927.

1907 MULLANY, Peter F. "Religion in Massinger's *The Maid of Honour.*" *RenD,* n.s. 2 (1969), 143–56.

1908 PHIALAS, Peter G. "Massinger and the *Commedia dell'Arte.*" *MLN,* 65 (1950), 113–4.

1909 PHIALAS, Peter G. "The Sources of Massinger's *Emperour of the East.*" *PMLA,* 65 (1950), 473–82.

1910 RAEBEL, K. *Massingers Drama 'The Maid of Honour' in seinem Verhältnis zu Painters 'Palace of Pleasure.'* Halle: H. John, 1901.

1911 RICE, Warner G. "The Source of Massinger's *The Renegado.*" *PQ,* 11 (1932), 65–75.

1912 SPENCER, Benjamin T. "Philip Massinger." *Seventeenth Century Studies.* Robert Shafer, ed. Princeton: Princeton University Press, 1933. Pp. 3–19.

1913 SYKES, H. Dugdale. "Massinger and Dekker's 'The Virgin Martyr.'" *N&Q,* 12 series 10 (1922), 61–5, 83–8.

1914 SYKES, H. Dugdale. "Massinger and *The Sea Voyage.*" *N&Q,* 12 Series 11 (1922), 443–46, 484–86.

1915 THOMSON, Patricia. "The Old Way and the New Way in Dekker and Massinger." *MLR,* 51 (1956), 168–78.

1916 WAITH, Eugene M. "*Controversia* in the English Drama: Medwall and Massinger." *PMLA,* 68 (1953), 286–303.

1917 WAITH, Eugene M. "The Sources of *The Double Marriage* by Fletcher and Massinger." *MLN,* 64 (1949), 505–10.

1918 YAMASHITA, Hiroshi. "The Printing of Phillip Massinger's Plays." *ShStud,* 10 (1971–72), 16–38.

Middleton, Thomas (1570?–1627)

Bibliography

1919 DONOVAN, Dennis, ed. *Thomas Middleton, 1939–1965; John Webster, 1940–1965.* Elizabethan Bibliographies Supplements 1. London: Nether Press, 1967.

Works

1920 *The Works of Thomas Middleton.* 8 vols. A. H. Bullen, ed. London: Bullen, 1885–86.

1921 *The Changeling.* N. W. Bawcutt, ed. Revels Plays. Cambridge: Harvard University Press, 1958.

1922 *The Changeling.* M. W. Black, ed. Philadelphia: University of Pennsylvania Press, 1966.

1923 *The Changeling.* G. W. Williams, ed. Regents Renaissance Drama Series. Lincoln: University of Nebraska Press, 1966.

1924 *A Chaste Maid in Cheapside.* C. L. Barber, ed. Fountainwell. Berkeley: University of California Press, 1969.

1925 *A Chaste Maid in Cheapside.* Alan Brissenden, ed. New Mermaids. New York: Hill & Wang, 1968.

1926 *A Chaste Maid in Cheapside.* R. B. Parker, ed. Revels Plays. Cambridge: Harvard University Press, 1969.

1927 *A Mad World, My Masters.* S. Henning, ed. Regents Renaissance Drama Series. Lincoln: University of Nebraska Press, 1965.

1928 *Michaelmas Term.* Richard Levin, ed. Regents Renaissance Drama Series. Lincoln: University of Nebraska Press, 1966.

1929 *A Trick to Catch the Old One.* C. L. Barber, ed. Fountainwell. Berkeley: University of California Press, 1968.

1930 *A Trick to Catch the Old One.* G. J. Watson, ed. New Mermaids. New York: HIll & Wang, 1968.

1931 *Women Beware Women.* C. L. Barber, ed. Fountainwell. Berkeley: University of California Press, 1969.

1932 *A Fair Quarrel.* Roger V. Holdsworth, ed. New Mermaids. London: Benn, 1974.

Studies

1933 ANDREWS, Michael C. " 'Sweetness' in *The Changeling.*" *YES,* 1 (1971), 63–7.

1934 ASP, Carolyn. *A Study of Thomas Middleton's Tragicomedies.* Jacobean Drama Studies 28. Salzburg: Institut für Englische Sprache und Literatur, Universität Salzburg, 1974.

1935 BAINES, Barbara J. *The Lust Motif in the Plays of Thomas Middleton.* Jacobean Drama Studies 29. Salzburg: Institut für Englische Sprache und Literatur, Universität Salzburg, 1973.

1936 BALD, R. C. "The Chronology of Thomas Middleton's Plays." *MLR,* 32 (1937), 33–43.

1937 BALD, R. C. "An Early Version of Middleton's *Game at Chesse.*" *MLR,* 38 (1943), 177–80.

1938 BALD, R. C. "Middleton's Civic Employments." *MP,* 31 (1933), 65–78.

1939 BARKER, Richard H. "The Authorship of the *Second Maiden's Tragedy* and *The Revenger's Tragedy.*" *SAB,* 20 (1945), 51–62, 121–33.

1940 BARKER, Richard H. *Thomas Middleton.* New York: Columbia University Press, 1958.

1941 BATCHELOR, J. B. "The Pattern of *Women Beware Women.*" *YES,* 2 (1972), 78–88.

1942 BERGER, Thomas L. "The Petrarchan Fortress of *The Changeling.*" *RenP 1969,* (1970), 37–46.

1943 BOWERS, Fredson T. "Middleton's *Fair Quarrel* and the Duelling Code." *JEGP,* 36 (1937), 40–65.

1944 BRADFORD, Gamaliel. "The Women of Middleton and Webster." *SR,* 29 (1921), 14–29.

1945 BRITTEN, Norman A. *Thomas Middleton.* New York: Twayne, 1972.

1946 BUCKINGHAM, Elizabeth Lee. "Campion's *Art of English Poesie* and Middleton's *Chaste Maid in Cheapside.*" *PMLA,* 43 (1928), 784–92.

1947 BULLOCK, Helene B. "Thomas Middleton and the Fashion in Playmaking." *PMLA,* 42 (1927), 766–76.

1948 BULLOUGH, Geoffrey. *The Game at Chesse:* How it Struck a Contemporary." *MLR,* 49 (1954), 156–63.

1949 BURELBACH, Frederick. "Theme and Structure in *The Spanish Gipsy.*" *HAB,* 19 (1968), 37–41.

1950 CHATTERJI, Ruby. "Theme, Imagery, and Unity in *A Chaste Maid in Cheapside.*" *RenD,* 8 (1965), 105–26.

1951 CHATTERJI, Ruby. "Unity and Disparity: *Michaelmas Term.*" *SEL,* 8 (1968), 349–63.

1952 CHERRY, Caroline L. *The Most Unvaluedst Purchase: Women in the Plays of Thomas Middleton.* Jacobean Drama Studies 34. Salzburg: Institut für Englische Sprache und Literatur, Universität Salzburg, 1973.

1953 CHRISTIAN, Mildred Gayler. "Middleton's Acquaintance with the *Merrie Conceited Jests of George Peele.*" *PMLA,* 50 (1935), 753–60.

1954 COPE, Jackson I. "The Date of Middleton's *Women Beware Women.*" *MLN,* 76 (1961), 295–300.

1955 CORE, George. "The Canker and The Muse: Imagery in *Women Beware Women.*" *RenP 1967,* (1968), 65–76.

1956 COVATTA, Anthony. "Remarriage in *Michaelmas Term.*" *N&Q,* n.s. 19 (1972), 460–1.

1957 COVATTA, Anthony. *Thomas Middleton's City Comedies.* Lewisburg, Pa.: Bucknell University Press, 1973.

1958 DAVIDSON, Clifford. "Middleton and the *Family of Love.*" *English Miscellany,* 20 (1969), 81–92.

1959 DAVIDSON, Clifford. "*The Phoenix:* Middleton's Didactic Comedy." *PLL,* 4 (1968), 121–30.

1960 DESSEN, Alan C. "Middleton's *The Phoenix* and the Allegorical Tradition." *SEL,* 6 (1966), 291–308.

1961 DOOB, Penelope B. R. "A Reading of *The Changeling.*" *ELR,* 3 (1973), 183–206.

1962 DUFFY, Joseph M. "Madhouse Optics: *The Changeling.*" *CompD,* 8 (1974), 184–98.

1963 DUNKEL, W. D. "The Authorship of *The Puritan.*" *PMLA,* 45 (1930), 804–8.

1964 DUNKEL, W. D. *The Dramatic Technique of Middleton in his Comedies of London Life.* Chicago: University of Chicago Press, 1925.

1965 ECCLES, Mark. "Middleton's Birth and Education." *RES,* 7 (1931), 431–41.

1966 ECCLES, Mark. "'Thomas Middleton a Poett.'" *SP,* 54 (1957), 516–36.

1967 EWBANK, Inga-Stina. "Realism and Morality in *Women Beware Women.*" *E&S 1969,* 57–70.

1968 FARR, Dorothy M. "*The Changeling.*" *MLR,* 62 (1967), 586–97.

1969 FARR, Dorothy M. *Thomas Middleton and the Drama of Realism: A Study of Some Representative Plays.* Edinburgh: Oliver & Boyd, 1973.

1970 GEORGE, David. "Thomas Middleton at Oxford." *MLR,* 65 (1970), 734–6.

1971 GEORGE, David. "Thomas Middleton's Sources: A Survey." *N&Q,* 216 (1971), 17–24.

1972 GIBBONS, Brian. **See 642.**

1973 GORDON, D. J. "Middleton's *No Wit, No Help Like a Woman's* and della Porta's *La Sorella.*" *RES,* 17 (1942), 400–14.

1974 HALLETT, Charles A. "Middleton's Allwit: The Urban Cynic." *MLQ*, 30 (1969), 498–507.

1975 HALLETT, Charles A. *Middleton's Cynics: A Study of Middleton's Insight into the Moral Psychology of the Mediocre Mind*. Jacobean Drama Studies 47. Salzburg: Institut für Englische Sprache und Literatur, Universität Salzburg, 1975.

1976 HALLETT, Charles A. "Middleton's Overreachers and the Ironic Ending." *TSL*, 16 (1971), 1–13.

1977 HALLETT, Charles A. "Penitent Brothel, the Succubus and Parson's *Resolution:* A Reappraisal of Penitent's Position in Middleton's Canon." *SP*, 69 (1972), 72–86.

1978 HALLETT, Charles A. "The Psychological Drama of *Women Beware Women.*" *SEL*, 12 (1972), 375–89.

1979 HÉBERT, Catherine. "A Note on the Significance of the Title of Middleton's *The Changeling.*" *CLAJ*, 12 (1968), 66–9.

1980 HEINEMANN, Margot C. "Middleton's *A Game at Chess:* Parliamentary-Puritans and Opposition Drama." *ELR*, 5 (1975), 232–50.

1981 HIBBARD, G. R. "The Tragedies of Thomas Middleton and the Decadence of the Drama." *RMS*, 1 (1957), 35–64.

1982 HOLMES, David M. *The Art of Thomas Middleton*. London: Oxford University Press, 1970.

1983 HOLZKNECHT, Karl J. "The Dramatic Structure of *The Changeling.*" *RenP 1953* (1954), 77–87.

1984 JACOBS, Henry E. "The Constancy of Change: Character and Perspective in *The Changeling.*" *TSLL*, 16 (1975), 651–74.

1985 JOHANNSON, B. *Law and Lawyers in Elizabethan England as Evidenced in the Plays of Ben Jonson and Thomas Middleton*. Stockholm: Stockholm Studies in English, 1967.

1986 JOHANNSON, B. *Religion and Superstition in the Plays of Ben Jonson and Thomas Middleton*. Upsala: A. B. Lundegnistska Bokhandeln, 1950.

1987 JORDAN, Robert. "Myth and Psychology in *The Changeling.*" *RenD*, n.s. 3 (1970), 157–66.

1988 JUMP, J. D. "Middleton's Tragedies." *The Age of Shakespeare*. Pelican Guide to English Literature 2. Baltimore: Penguin, 1955. Pp. 355–68.

1989 KISTNER, Arthur L. and M. K. KISTNER. "*The Spanish Gipsy.*" *HAB*, 25 (1974), 211–24.

1990 LAWRENCE, Robert G. "A Bibliographical Study of Middleton and Rowley's *The Changeling.*" *The Library*, 5th series 16 (1961), 37–43.

1991 LEVIN, Richard. "The Dampit Scenes in *A Trick to Catch the Old One.*" *MLQ*, 25 (1964), 140–52.

1992 LEVIN, Richard. "The Three Quarrels of *A Fair Quarrel.*" *SP*, 61 (1964), 219–31.

1993 McELROY, John F. *Parody and Burlesque in the Tragicomedies of Thomas Middleton*. Jacobean Drama Studies 19. Salzburg: Institut für Englische Sprache und Literatur, Universität Salzburg, 1972.

1994 MAROTTI, Arthur F. "Fertility and Comic Form in *A Chaste Maid in Cheapside.*" *CompD*, 3 (1969), 65–74.

1995　MAROTTI, Arthur F. "The Method in the Madness of *A Mad World, My Masters.*" *TSL,* 15 (1970), 99–108.

1996　MAROTTI, Arthur F. "The Purgations of Middleton's *The Family of Love.*" *PLL,* 7 (1971), 80–4.

1997　MAXWELL, Baldwin. "Middleton's *Michaelmas Term.*" *PQ,* 22 (1943), 29–35.

1998　MAXWELL, Baldwin. "Middleton's *The Phoenix.*" *Joseph Quincy Adams: Memorial Studies.* Pp. 743–53. **See 289.**

1999　MAXWELL, Baldwin. "Thomas Middleton's *Your Five Gallants.*" *PQ,* 30 (1951), 30–9.

2000　MOORE, John Robert. "The Contemporary Significance of Middleton's *Game at Chesse.*" *PMLA,* 50 (1935), 761–8.

2001　MULRYNE, J. R. "The French Source for the Sub-Plot of Middleton's *Women Beware Women. RES,* 25 (1974), 439–45.

2002　MULRYNE, J. R. "Manuscript Source—Material for the Main Plot of Thomas Middleton's *Women Beware Women.*" *YES,* 5 (1975), 70–4.

2003　PARKER, R. B. "Middleton's Experiments with Comedy and Judgement." *Jacobean Theatre.* Pp. 179–200. **See 276.**

2004　PASTER, Gail K. "The City in Plautus and Middleton." *RenD,* 6 (1973), 29–44.

2005　PENTZELL, Raymond J. "*The Changeling:* Notes on Mannerism in Dramatic Form." *CompD,* 9 (1975), 3–28.

2006　PHIALAS, Peter G. "Middleton's Early Contact with the Law." *SP,* 52 (1955), 186–94.

2007　PRICE, George R. "The First Edition of *Your Five Gallants* and of *Michaelmas Term.*" *The Library,* 5th series, 8 (1953), 23–29.

2008　PRICE, George R. "The Huntington MS of *A Game at Chesse.*" *HLQ,* 17 (1953), 83–8.

2009　PRICE, George R. "The Latin Oration in *A Game at Chesse.*" *HLQ,* 23 (1960), 389–93.

2010　PUTT, S. Gorley. "The Tormented World of Middleton." *TLS,* 2 August (1974), 833–4.

2011　RICKS, Christopher. "The Moral and Poetical Structure of *The Changeling.*" *EIC,* 10 (1960), 290–306.

2012　RICKS, Christopher. "Word-Play in *Women Beware Women.*" *RES,* 12 (1961), 238–50.

2013　ROWE, George E., Jr. "*The Old Law* and Middleton's Comic Vision." *ELH,* 42 (1975), 189–202.

2014　SARGENT, Roussel. "Theme and Structure in Middleton's *A Game at Chess.*" *MLR,* 66 (1971), 721–30.

2015　SCHOENBAUM, S. "*A Chaste Maid in Cheapside* and Middleton's City Comedy." *Studies in the English Renaissance Drama.* Pp. 287–309. **See 270.**

2016　SCHOENBAUM, S. "*Hengist, King of Kent* and Sexual Preoccupation in Jacobean Drama." *PQ,* 29 (1950), 182–98.

2017　SCHOENBAUM, S. *Middleton's Tragedies: A Critical Study.* New York: Columbia University Press, 1955.

2018 SCHOENBAUM, S. "Middleton's Tragicomedies." *MP*, 54 (1956), 7–19.

2019 SLIGHTS, William W. E. "The Trickster-Hero and Middleton's *A Mad World, My Masters.*" *CompD*, 8 (1965), 105–26.

2020 SOUTHALL, R. "A Missing Source-Book for Middleton's *A Game at Chesse.*" *N&Q*, n.s. 9 (1962), 145–6.

2021 STAGG, Louis C. *An Index to the Figurative Language of Thomas Middleton's Tragedies.* Charlottesville: Bibliographical Society of the University of Virginia, 1970.

2022 TAYLOR, J. Chesley. "Metaphors of the Moral World: Structure in *The Changeling.*" *Tulane Studies in English* 20 (1970), 41–56.

2023 TEAGARDEN, Lucetta J. "The Dekker-Middleton Problem in *Michaelmas Term.*" *UTSE,* 26 (1947), 49–58.

2024 WADSWORTH, F. W. *"The Revenger's Tragedy."* *MLR,* 50 (1955), 307.

2025 WIGLER, Stephen. "Penitent Brothel Reconsidered: The Place of the Grotesque in Middleton's *A Mad World, My Masters.*" *Literature and Psychology,* 25 (1975), 17–26.

2026 WILLIAMS, Robert I. "Machiavelli's *Mandragola,* Touchwood Senior, and the Comedy of Middleton's *A Chaste Maid at Cheapside.*" *SEL,* 10 (1970), 385–96.

Peele, George (1558?–1597?)

Bibliography

2027 JOHNSON, ed. **See 1052.**

Works

2028 *The Dramatic Works of George Peele.* 3 vols. C. T. Prouty, gen. ed. New Haven: Yale University Press, 1952–1970.

Studies

2029 ADAMS, Charles S. "The Tales in Peele's *Old Wives' Tale.*" *Midwest Folklore,* 13 (1963), 13–20.

2030 ASHLEY, L. R. N. *Authorship and Evidence: A Study of Attribution and the Renaissance Drama, Illustrated by The Case of George Peele 1556–1596.* Études de Philologie et d'Histoire 6. Geneva: Droz, 1968.

2031 ASHLEY, L. R. N. George Peele. New York: Twayne, 1970.

2032 BLAIR, Carolyn. "On the Question of Unity in Peele's *David and Bethsabe.*" *Studies in Honor of John C. Hodges and Alwin Thaler.* R. B. Davis and J. L. Lievsay, eds. Knoxville: University of Tennessee Press. Pp. 35–41.

2033 BRADBROOK, M. C. "Peele's *Old Wives' Tale:* A Play of Enchantment." *ES,* 63 (1962), 323–30.

2034 BRINKMANN, H. *Die dramatische Kunst in George Peele's Arraignment of Paris.* Münster: Lengerich i. W., Handelsdruck, 1938.

2035 CHEFFAUD, P. H. *George Peele (1558–1596?).* Paris: F. Alcan, 1913.

2036 CLAPP, Sarah Lewis Carol. "Peele's Use of Folk Lore in *The Old Wives' Tale.*" *UTSE.* 6 (1926), 146–56.

2037 DeSTASIO, Clotilde. "Il linguaggio drammatico di George Peele." *English Miscellany,* 15 (1964), 61–87.

2038 DOEBLER, John. "The Tone of George Peele's *The Old Wives' Tale.*" *ES,* 53 (1972), 412–21.

2039 EWBANK (née Ekeblad), Inga-Stina. "The House of David in Renaissance Drama: A Comparative Study." *RenD,* 8 (1965), 3–40.

2040 EWBANK, Inga-Stina. "*The Love of King David and Fair Bethsabe;* A Note on George Peele's Biblical Drama." *ES,* 39 (1958), 57–62.

2041 EWBANK, Inga-Stina. "On the Background of Peele's *Araygnment of Paris.*" *N&Q,* n.s. 3 (1956), 246–9.

2042 EWBANK, Inga-Stina. " 'What words, what looks, what wonders?' " Language and Spectacle in the Theatre of George Peele." *The Elizabethan Theatre V.* Pp. 124–54. **See 286.**

2043 GELBER, Mark. "The Unity of George Peele's *The Old Wives' Tale.*" *New York-Pennsylvania MLA Newsletter,* 2 (1969), 3–9.

2044 GOLDSTONE, Herbert. "Interplay in Peele's *The Old Wives' Tale.*" *BUSE,* 4 (1960), 202–13.

2045 HORNE, D. H. *The Life and Minor Works of George Peele.* New Haven: Yale University Press, 1953.

2046 JEFFERY, Violet M. "Italian and English Pastoral Drama of the Renaissance: The Source of Peele's *Arraignment of Paris.*" *MLR,* 19 (1924), 175–87.

2047 JENKINS, Harold. "Peele's *Old Wives' Tale.*" *MLR,* 34 (1939), 177–85.

2048 JONES, Gwynan. "The Intention of Peele's *Old Wives' Tale.*" *Aberystwyth Studies,* 7 (1926), 79–93.

2049 LARSEN, Thorleif. "A Bibliography of the Writings of George Peele." *MP,* 32 (1934), 143–56.

2050 LARSEN, Thorleif. "The Canon of Peele's Works." *MP,* 36 (1928), 191–99.

2051 LARSON, Thorleif. "The Early Years of George Peele, Dramatist, 1558–1588." *PTRSC,* 22 (1928), sec. ii:271–318.

2052 LESNICK, Henry G. "The Structural Significance of Myth and Flattery in Peele's *Arraignment of Paris.*" *SP,* 65 (1968), 163–70.

2053 REEVES, J. D. "The Cause of the Trojan War According to Peele." *N&Q,* 200 (1955), 333.

2054 RIBNER, Irving. "Shakespeare and Peele: The Death of Cleopatra." *N&Q,* 198 (1952), 244–6.

2055 ROCKEY, Laurilyn J. "*The Old Wives' Tale* As Dramatic Satire." *ETJ,* 22 (1970), 268–75.

2056 SAMPLEY, Arthur M. "Plot Structure in Peele's Plays as a Test of Authorship." *PMLA,* 51 (1936), 689–701.

2057 SAMPLEY, Arthur M. "The Text of Peele's *David and Bethsabe.*" *PMLA,* 46 (1931), 659–71.

2058 SENN, Werner. *Studies in the Dramatic Construction of Robert Greene and George Peele.* Bern: Francke, 1973.

2059 Von HENDY, Andrew. "The Triumph of Chastity: Form and Meaning in *The Arraignment of Paris.*" *RenD,* n.s. 1 (1968), 87–101.

Shirley, James (1596–1666)

Bibliography

2060 PENNEL, and Williams, eds. See **748.**

Works

2061 *The Dramatic Works and Poems of James Shirley.* 6 vols. William Gifford and Alexander Dyce, eds. London: John Murray, 1833. Reprinted, New York: Russell & Russell, 1966.

2062 *The Cardinal.* Charles R. Forker, ed. Indiana University Humanities Series 56. Bloomington: Indiana University Press, 1964.

2063 *The Traitor.* J. S. Carter, ed. Regents Renaissance Drama Series. Lincoln: University of Nebraska Press, 1965.

Studies

2064 BAS, Georges. "James Shirley, pasteur dans le Hertfordshire." *EA,* 15 (1962), 266–8.

2065 BAUGH, Albert C. "Further Facts about James Shirley." *RES,* 7 (1931), 62–6.

2066 BAUGH, Albert C. "Some New Facts About Shirley." *MLR,* 17 (1922), 228–35.

2067 CRAWLEY, Derek. "The Effect of Shirley's Hand on Chapman's *The Tragedy of Chabot Admiral of France.*" *SP,* 63 (1966), 677–96.

2068 CRINÒ, Anna Maria. *James Shirley; drammaturgo di corte.* Verona: Ghidini, 1968.

2069 FEIL, J. P. "James Shirley's Years of Service." *RES,* 8 (1957), 413–6.

2070 FORKER, Charles R. "Shirley's *The Cardinal:* Some Problems and Cruces." *N&Q,* n.s. 6 (1959), 232–3

2071 FORSYTHE, Robert S. *The Relations of Shirley's Plays to the Elizabethan Drama.* New York: Columbia University Press, 1914.

2072 HARBAGE, Alfred B. "The Authorship of the Dramatic *Arcadia.*" *PMLA,* 35 (1938), 233–7.

2073 HOGAN, A. P. "Thematic Analysis of *The Cardinal:* A New Perspective on Shirley." *YES,* 5 (1975), 75–85.

2074 McGRATH, Juliet. "James Shirley's Uses of 'Language'." *SEL,* 6 (1966), 323–39.

2075 MacMULLEN, Hugh. "The Sources of Shirley's 'St. Patrick for Ireland'." *PMLA,* 48 (1933), 806–14.

2076 MORILLO, Marvin. "Shirley's 'Preferment' and the Court of Charles I." *SEL*, 1 (1961), 101–17.

2077 MORTON, Richard: "Deception and Social Dislocation: An Aspect of James Shirley's Drama." *RenD*, 9 (1966), 227–46.

2078 NASON, Arthur. *James Shirley, Dramatist: A Biographical and Critical Study.* New York: A. H. Nason, 1915.

2079 REED, Robert R., Jr. "James Shirley, and the Sentimental Comedy." *Anglia*, 73 (1955), 149–70.

2080 RIEMER, A. P. "A Source for Shirley's *The Traitor.*" *RES*, 14 (1963), 380–3.

2081 SENSABAUGH, G. F. "Platonic Love in Shirley's *The Lady of Pleasure.*" *A Tribute to George Coffin Taylor.* Chapel Hill: University of North Carolina Press, 1952. Pp. 168–77.

2082 STADTFELD, Frieder, " '*Fortune*', '*providence*' und '*manners*' in James Shirley's *Hyde Park.*" *Anglia*, 93 (1975), 111–39.

2083 STEVENSON, Allan H. "James Shirley and the Actors of the First Irish Theater." *MP*, 40 (1942), 147–60.

2084 STEVENSON, Allan H. "Shirley's Years in Ireland." *RES*, 20 (1944), 19–28.

2084A WERTHEIM, Albert. "Games and Courtship in James Shirley's *Hyde Park.*" *Anglia*, 90 (1972), 71–91.

2085 WERTHEIM, Albert. "James Shirley and the Caroline Masques of Ben Jonson." *TN*, 27 (1973), 157–61.

Tourneur, Cyril (Died 1626)

Bibliography

2086 DONOVAN, ed. See **926.**

Works

2087 *The Works of Cyril Tourneur.* Allardyce Nicoll, ed. London: Fanfrolico Press, 1930. Reprinted, New York: Russell & Russell, 1963.

2088 *The Plays and Poems of Cyril Tourneur.* John Churton Collins, ed. London: Chatto & Windus, 1878.

2089 *The Atheist's Tragedy.* Irving Ribner, ed. The Revels Plays. Cambridge: Harvard University Press, 1964.

2090 *The Revenger's Tragedy.* R. A. Foakes, ed. Revels Plays. Cambridge: Harvard University Press, 1966.

2091 *The Revenger's Tragedy.* B. Gibbons, ed. New Mermaids. New York: Hill & Wang, 1967.

2092 *The Revenger's Tragedy.* Lawrence J. Ross, ed. Regents Renaissance Drama Series. Lincoln: University of Nebraska Press, 1966.

Studies

2093 ADAMS, H. H. "Cyril Tourneur on Revenge." *JEGP,* 48 (1949), 72–87.

2094 AYRES, Philip J. "Parallel Action and Reductive Technique in *The Revenger's Tragedy.*" *ELN,* 8 (1970), 103–7

2095 CAMOIN, François A. *The Revenge Convention of Tourneur, Webster and Middleton.* Jacobean Drama Studies 20. Salzburg: Institut für Englische Sprache und Literatur, Universität Salzburg, 1972.

2096 CHAMPION, Larry S. "Tourneur's *The Revenger's Tragedy* and the Jacobean Tragic Perspective." *SP,* 72 (1975), 299–321.

2097 COPE, Jackson I. "Tourneur's *Atheist's Tragedy* and the Jig of 'Singing Simkin.' " *MLN,* 70 (1955), 571–3.

2098 DUNKEL, W. D. "The Authorship of *The Revenger's Tragedy.*" *PMLA,* 46 (1931), 781–5.

2099 ELLIS-FERMOR, Una M. "The Imagery of *The Revenger's Tragedie* and *The Atheist's Tragedie.*" *MLR,* 30 (1935), 289–301.

2100 EWBANK (née Ekeblad), Inga-Stina. "An Approach to Tourneur's Imagery." *MLR,* 54 (1959), 489–98.

2101 EWBANK, Inga-Stina. "On the Authorship of *The Revenger's Tragedy.*" *ES,* 41 (1960), 225–40.

2102 EWBANK, Inga-Stina. "A Note on *The Revenger's Tragedy.*" *N&Q,* 200 (1955), 98–9.

2103 FOAKES, R. A. "The Art of Cruelty: Hamlet and Vindice." *SS,* 26 (1973), 21–32.

2104 FOAKES, R. A. "On the Authorship of *The Revenger's Tragedy.*" *MLR,* 48 (1953), 129–38.

2105 GECKLE, George L. "Justice in *The Revenger's Tragedy.*" *RenP 1073* (1974), 75–82.

2106 HIGGINS, Michael H. "The Influence of Calvinistic Thought in Tourneur's *Atheist's Tragedy.*" *RES,* 19 (1943), 255–62.

2107 HUNTER, G. K. "A Source for *The Revenger's Tragedy.*" *RES,* 10 (1959), 181–2.

2108 JACOBSON, Daniel Jonathan. *The Language of "The Revenger's Tragedy."* Jacobean Drama Studies 38. Salzburg: Institut für Englische Sprache und Literatur, Universität Salzburg, 1974.

2109 JENKINS, Harold. "Cyril Tourneur." *RES,* 17 (1941), 21–36.

2110 KAUFMANN, R. J. "Theodicy, Tragedy and the Psalmist: Tourneur's *Atheist's Tragedy.*" *CompD,* 3 (1969–70), 241–62.

2111 KISTNER, Arthur L., and M. K. KISTNER. "Morality and Inevitability in *The Revenger's Tragedy.*" *JEGP,* 71 (1972), 36–46.

2112 LAYMAN, B. J. "Tourneur's Artificial Noon: The Design of *The Revenger's Tragedy.*" *MLQ,* 34 (1973), 20–35.

2113 LEECH, Clifford. "*The Atheist's Tragedy* as a Dramatic Comment on Chapman's *Bussy* Plays." *JEGP,* 52 (1953), 525–30.

2114 LEGOUIS, Pierre. "Réflexions sur la recherche des sources à propos de la *Tragedie du vengeur.*" *EA,* 12 (1959), 47–55.

2115 LISCA, Peter. "*The Revenger's Tragedy:* A Study in Irony." *PQ,* 38 (1959), 242–51.

2116 LOCKERT, Lacy. "The Greatest of Elizabethan Melodramas." *Essays in Dramatic Literature.* Pp. 103–26. **See 279.**

2117 MURRAY, Peter B. "The Authorship of *The Revenger's Tragedy.*" *PBSA,* 56 (1962), 195–218.

2118 MURRAY, Peter B. *A Study of Cyril Tourneur.* Philadelphia: University of Pennsylvania Press, 1964.

2119 NICOLL, Allardyce. "*The Revenger's Tragedy* and the Virtue of Anonymity." *Essays on Shakespeare and Elizabethan Drama.* Pp. 309–16. **See 287.**

2120 OLIPHANT, E. H. C. "The Authorship of *The Revenger's Tragedy.*" *SP,* 23 (1926), 157–68.

2121 OLIPHANT, E. H. C. "Tourneur and Mr. Eliot." *SP,* 32 (1935), 346–52.

2122 ORNSTEIN, Robert. "*The Atheist's Tragedy.*" *N&Q,* 200 (1955), 284–5.

2123 ORNSTEIN, Robert. "*The Atheist's Tragedy* and Renaissance Naturalism." *SP,* 51 (1954), 194–207.

2124 ORNSTEIN, Robert. "The Ethical Design of *The Revenger's Tragedy.*" *ELH,* 21 (1954), 81–93.

2125 PETER, John. "*The Revenger's Tragedy* Reconsidered." *EIC,* 6 (1956), 131–43.

2126 PRICE, George R. "The Authorship and Bibliography of *The Revenger's Tragedy.*" *The Library,* n.s. 15 (1960), 262–77.

2127 SALINGAR, L. G. "*The Revenger's Tragedy* and the Morality Tradition." *Scrutiny,* 11 (1938), 402–24.

2128 SALINGAR, L. G. "Tourneur and *The Tragedy of Revenge.*" *The Age of Shakespeare.* Penguin Guide to English Literature 2. Baltimore: Penguin, 1955. Pp. 334–54.

2129 SANDERS, L. "*The Revenger's Tragedy:* A Play on the Revenge Play." *Renaissance & Reformation,* 10 (1974), 25–36.

2130 SCHOENBAUM, S. "*The Revenger's Tragedy:* Jacobean Dance of Death." *MLQ,* 15 (1954), 201–7.

2131 SCHOENBAUM, S. "*The Revenger's Tragedy* and Middleton's Moral Outlook." *N&Q,* 196 (1951), 8–10.

2132 STAGG, Louis C. *An Index to the Figurative Language of Civil Tourneur's Tragedies.* Charlottesville: Bibliographical Society of the University of Virginia, 1970.

2133 STERNLICHT, Sanford. "Tourneur's Imagery and *The Revenger's Tragedy.*" *PLL,* 6 (1970), 192–7.

2134 TOMLINSON, T. B. "The Morality of Revenge: Tourneur's Critics." *EIC,* 10 (1960), 134–47.

2135 TOMPKINS, J. M. S. "Tourneur and the Stars." *RES,* 22 (1946), 315–9.

2136 WALLER, G. F. "Time, Providence and Tragedy in *The Atheist's Tragedy* and *King Lear.*" *English Miscellany,* 23 (1972), 55–74.

2137 WIGLER, Stephen. " 'If Looks Could Kill' Fathers and Sons in *The Revenger's Tragedy.*" *CompD,* 9 (1975), 206–25.

2138 WILDS, Nancy G. " 'Of Rare Fire Compact': Image and Rhetoric in *The Revenger's Tragedy.*" *TSLL,* 17 (1975), 61–74.

Udall, Nicholas (1505–1556)

Studies

2139 BRADNER, Leicester. "A Test for Udall's Authorship." *MLN,* 42 (1927), 278–80.

2140 BYROM, H. J. "Some Lawsuits of Nicholas Udall." *RES,* 11 (1935), 457–9.

2141 CARPENTER, Nan Cooke. "*Ralph Roister Doister:* Miles versus Clericus." *N&Q,* n.s. 7 (1960), 168–70.

2142 EDGERTON, William L. "The Apostasy of Nicholas Udall." *N&Q,* 195 (1950), 223–6.

2143 EDGERTON, William L. "Nicholas Udall in the Indexes of Prohibited Books." *JEGP,* 55 (1956), 247–52.

2144 HINTON, J. S. "The Source of *Roister Doister.*" *MP,* 11 (1913–14), 273–8.

2145 MILLER, Edwin Shephard. "Roister Doister's 'Euneralls'." *SP,* 43 (1946), 42–58.

2146 PEERY, William. "Udall as Timeserver." *N&Q,* 194 (1949), 119–21.

2147 PLUMSTEAD, A. W. "Satirical Parody in *Roister Doister:* A Reinterpretation." *SP,* 60 (1963), 141–54.

2148 PLUMSTEAD, A. W. "Who Pointed Roister's Letter?" *N&Q,* n.s. 10 (1963), 329–31.

2149 REED, Arthur W. "Nicholas Udall and Thomas Wilson." *RES,* 1 (1925), 275–83.

2150 WEBSTER, Herbert T. "*Ralph Roister Doister* and the Little Eyases." *N&Q,* 196 (1951), 135–6.

Webster, John (1580?–1625?)

Bibliography

2151 DONOVAN, ed. See **1919.**

2152 MAHANEY, William E., ed. *John Webster: A Classified Bibliography.* Jacobean Drama Studies 10. Salzburg: Institut für Englische Sprache und Literatur, Universität Salzburg, 1973.

Works

2153 *The Complete Works of John Webster.* 4 vols. F. L. Lucas, ed. London: Chatto & Windus, 1927.

2154 *The Devil's Law Case.* F. A. Shirley, ed. Regents Renaissance Drama Series. Lincoln: University of Nebraska Press, 1972.

2156 *The Duchess of Malfi.* Elizabeth M. Brennan, ed. New Mermaids. New York: Hill & Wang, 1966.

2157 *The Duchess of Malfi.* John Russell Brown, ed. Revels Plays. Cambridge: Harvard University Press, 1964.

2158 *The White Devil.* John Russell Brown, ed. Revels Plays. Cambridge: Harvard University Press, 1960.

2159 *The White Devil.* C. Hart, ed. Fountainwell. Berkeley: University of California Press, 1970.

2160 *The White Devil.* J. R. Mulryne, ed. Regents Renaissance Drama Series. Lincoln: University of Nebraska Press, 1969.

Studies

2161 AKRIGG, G. P. V. "John Webster and *The Book of Homilies.*" *N&Q,* n.s. 6 (1959) 217-8.

2162 ALLISON, Alexander W. "Ethical Themes in *The Duchess of Malfi.*" *SEL,* 4 (1964), 263-73.

2163 ANDERSON, Marcia Lee. "Webster's Debt to Guazzo." *SP,* 36 (1939), 192-205.

2164 ANSARI, K. H. *John Webster: Image Patterns and Canon.* Mystic, Conn.: Verry, 1969.

2165 BERLIN, Normand. "*The Duchess of Malfi:* Act V and Genre." *Genre,* 3 (1970), 351-63.

2166 BERRY, Ralph. *The Art of John Webster.* Oxford: The Clarendon Press, 1972.

2167 BODTKE, Richard. *Tragedy and the Jacobean Temper: The Major Plays of John Webster.* Jacobean Drama Studies 2. Salzburg: Institut für Englische Sprache und Literatur, Universität Salzburg, 1972.

2168 BOGARD, Gunnar. *The Tragic Satire of John Webster.* Berkeley: University of California Press, 1955.

2169 BOKLUND, Gunnar. *The Duchess of Malfi: Sources, Themes, Characters.* Cambridge: Harvard University Press, 1962.

2170 BOKLUND, Gunnar. *The Sources of The White Devil.* Cambridge: Harvard University Press, 1957.

2171 BRADFORD, Gamaliel. "The Women of Middleton and Webster." *SR,* 29 (1921), 14-29.

2172 BRENNAN, Elizabeth M. "The Relationship Between Brother and Sister in the Plays of John Webster." *MLR,* 58 (1963), 488-94.

2173 BROOKE, Rupert. *John Webster and the Elizabethan Drama.* New York: John Lane, 1916.

2174 BROWN, John Russell. "On the Dating of Webster's *The White Devil* and *The Duchess of Malfi.*" *PQ,* 31 (1952), 353–62.

2175 BROWN, John Russell. "The Printing of John Webster's Plays (I)." *SB,* 6 (1953), 117–140.

2176 CALDERWOOD, James L. "*The Duchess of Malfi:* Styles of Ceremony." *EIC,* 12 (1962), 133–47.

2177 CHAMPION, Larry S. "Webster's *The White Devil* and the Jacobean Tragic Perspective." *TSLL,* 16 (1974), 447–62.

2178 DALLBY, Anders. *The Anatomy of Evil: A Study of John Webster's "The White Devil".* Lund Studies in English 48. Lund: Gleerup, 1974.

2179 DAVIES, Cecil W. "The Structure of *The Duchess of Malfi:* An Approach." *English,* 12 (1958), 89–93.

2180 DAVISON, Richard A. "John Webster's Moral View Reexamined." *MSpr,* 63 (1969), 213–23.

2181 DENT, Robert W. *John Webster's Borrowing.* Berkeley: University of California Press, 1960.

2182 DENT, Robert W. "John Webster's Debt to William Alexander." *MLN,* 65 (1950), 73–82.

2183 DENT, Robert W. "Pierre Matthieu: Another Source for Webster." *HLQ* 17 (1953), 75–82.

2184 DENT, Robert W. "The White Devil, or Vittoria Corombona?" *RenD,* 9 (1966), 163–78.

2185 DRISCOLL, James P. "Integrity of Life in *The Duchess of Malfi.*" *Dramas,* 6 (1967), 42–53.

2186 DWYER, William W. *A Study of Webster's Use of Renaissance Natural and Moral Philosophy.* Jacobean Drama Studies 18. Salzburg: Institut für Englische Sprache und Literatur, Universität Salzburg, 1973.

2187 EDWARDS, W. A. "John Webster." *Determinations.* F. R. Leavis, ed. London: Chatto & Windus, 1934. Pp. 155–78.

2188 EKEBLAD, Inga-Stina. "The 'Impure Art' of John Webster." *RES,* 9 (1958), 235–67.

2189 EKEBLAD, Inga-Stina. "Webster's Constructional Rhythm." *ELH,* 24 (1957), 165–76.

2190 EMSLIE, McDonald. "Motives in Malfi." *EIC,* 9 (1959), 391–405.

2191 FIELER, Frank B. "The Eight Madmen in *The Duchess of Malfi.*" *SEL,* 7 (1967), 343–50.

2192 FORKER, Charles R. "Love, Death, and Fame: The Grotesque Tragedy of John Webster." *Anglia,* 91 (1973), 194–218.

2193 FORKER, Charles R. " 'Wit's Descant on any Plain Song': The Prose Characters of John Webster." *MLQ,* 30 (1969), 33–52.

2194 FRANKLIN, H. Bruce. "The Trial Scene of Webster's *The White Devil* Examined in Terms of Renaissance Rhetoric." *SEL,* 1 (1961), 35–51.

2195 GIANNETTI, Louis D. "A Contemporary View of *The Duchess of Malfi.*" *CompD,* 3 (1969–70), 297–307.

2196 GOREAU, Eloise. *Integrity of Life: Allegorical Imagery in the Plays of John Webster.* Jacobean Drama Studies 32. Salzburg: Institut für Englische Sprache und Literatur, Universität Salzburg, 1974.

2197 GRIFFIN, Robert P. *John Webster: Politics and Tragedy.* Jacobean Drama Studies 12. Salzburg: Institut für Englische Sprache und Literatur, Universität Salzburg, 1972.

2198 GUNBY, D. C. "*The Devil's Law Case:* An Interpretation." *MLR,* 63 (1968), 545–58.

2199 GUNBY, D. C. *Webster: The White Devil.* Studies in English Literature 45. London: Edward Arnold, 1971.

2200 HENDY, E. W. "John Webster: Playwright and Naturalist." *Nineteenth Century,* 103 (1928), 111–23.

2201 HENKE, James T. "John Webster's Motif of 'Consuming': An Approach to the Dramatic Unity and Tragic Vision of *The White Devil* and *The Duchess of Malfi.*" *Neuphilologische Mitteilungen* 76 (1975), 625–41.

2202 HOLLAND, George. "The Function of the Minor Characters in *The White Devil.*" *PQ,* 52 (1973), 43–54.

2203 HUNTER, G. K., and S. K. Hunter, eds. *John Webster: A Critical Anthology.* Harmondsworth, Essex: Penguin Books, 1969.

2204 HURT, James R. "Inverted Rituals in Webster's *The White Devil.*" *JEGP,* 61 (1962), 42–7.

2205 JACK, Ian. "The Case of John Webster." *Scrutiny,* 16 (1949), 38–43.

2206 JENKINS, Harold. "The Tragedy of Revenge in Shakespeare and Webster." *SS,* 14 (1961), 45–55.

2207 KNIGHT, G. Wilson. "*The Duchess of Malfi.*" *MHRev,* 4 (1967), 88–113.

2208 KROLL, Norma. "The Democritean Universe in Webster's *The White Devil.*" *CompD,* 7 (1973), 3–21.

2209 LAYMAN, B. J. "The Equilibrium of Opposites in *The White Devil:* A Reinterpretation." *PMLA,* 74 (1959), 336–47.

2210 LEECH, Clifford. *John Webster, A Critical Study.* London: The Hogarth Press, 1951.

2211 LEECH, Clifford. *Webster: The Duchess of Malfi.* London: Edward Arnold, 1963.

2212 LOCKERT, Lacy. "Marston, Webster, and the Decline of the Elizabethan Drama." *SR,* 27 (1919), 62–81.

2213 LOFTIS, John. "*The Duchess of Malfi* on the Spanish and English Stages." *RORD,* 12 (1969), 25–31.

2214 LUECKE, Jane Marie. "*The Duchess of Malfi:* Comic and Satiric Confusion in Tragedy." *SEL,* 4 (1964), 275–90.

2215 MAHANEY, William E. *Deception in the John Webster Plays: An Analytical Study.* Jacobean Drama Studies 9. Salzburg: Institut für Englische Sprache und Literatur, Universität Salzburg, 1973.

2216 MITCHELL, Giles, & Eugene P. WRIGHT. "Duke Ferdinand's Lycanthropy as a Disguise Motive in Webster's *The Duchess of Malfi.*" *Literature and Psychology,* 25 (1975), 117–23.

2217 MOORE, Don D. *John Webster and His Critics 1617–1964*. Baton Rouge: Louisiana State University Press, 1966.

2218 MULRYNE, J. R. *"The White Devil* and *The Duchess of Malfi." Jacobean Theatre.* Pp. 201–26. **See 276.**

2219 MURRAY, Peter B. *A Study of John Webster.* The Hague: Mouton, 1969.

2220 PRATT, Samuel M. "Webster's *The White Devil, V.* iv. 115." *Explicator,* 29 (1970), item 11.

2221 PRAZ, Mario. *Il dramma elisabettiano: Webster—Ford.* Roma: Edizioni Italiane "Studium Orbis," 1946.

2222 PRAZ, Mario. "John Webster and *The Maid's Tragedy." ES,* 37 (1956), 252–8.

2223 PRICE, Hereward T. "The Function of Imagery in Webster." *PMLA,* 70 (1955), 717–39.

2224 RIBNER, Irving. "Webster's Italian Tragedies." *TDR,* 5 (1961), 106–18.

2225 SEIDEN, Melvin. *The Revenge Motive in Websterean Tragedy.* Jacobean Drama Studies 15. Salzburg: Institut für Englische Sprache und Literatur, Universität Salzburg, 1973.

2226 SHUMAN, Samuel. "The Ring and the Jewel in Webster's Tragedies." *TSLL,* 14 (1972–73), 253–68.

2227 STERNLICHT, Sanford. *John Webster's Imagery and the Webster Canon.* Jacobean Drama Studies 1. Salzburg: Institut für Englische Sprache und Literatur, Universität Salzburg, 1972.

2228 STODDER, Joseph Henry. *Moral Perspective in Webster's Major Tragedies.* Jacobean Drama Studies 48. Salzburg: Institut für Englische Sprache und Literatur, Universität Salzburg, 1974.

2229 STOLL, E. E. *John Webster: The Periods of His Work.* Boston: A Mudge, 1905.

2230 SULLIVAN, S. W. "The Tendency to Rationalize in *The White Devil* and *The Duchess of Malfi." YES,* 4 (1974), 77–84.

2231 THAYER, C. G. "The Ambiguity of Bosola." *SP,* 54 (1957), 162–71.

2232 VERNON, P. F. "The Duchess of Malfi's Guilt." *N&Q* n.s. 10 (1963), 335–8.

2233 WADSWORTH, F. W. "Webster's *Duchess of Malfi* in the Light of Some Contemporary Ideas on Marriage and Remarriage." *PQ,* 35 (1956), 394–407.

2234 WEST, Muriel. *The Devil and John Webster.* Jacobean Drama Studies 11. Salzburg: Institut für Englische Sprache und Literatur, Universität Salzburg, 1974.

2235 WHITMAN, Robert T. *Beyond Melancholy: John Webster and The Tragedy of Darkness.* Jacobean Drama Studies 4. Salzburg: Institut für Englische Sprache und Literatur, Universität Salzburg, 1973.

2236 WHITMAN, Robert F. "The Moral Parodox of Webster's Tragedy." *PMLA,* 90 (1975), 894–903.

Masques, Pageants and Folk Drama

2237 *English Masques.* Herbert Arthur Evans, ed. London and Glasgow: Blackie & Son, 1897.

2238 *A Book of Masques: In Honour of Allardyce Nicoll.* T. J. B. Spencer *et al.,* eds. Cambridge: Cambridge University Press, 1964.

2239 *Designs by Inigo Jones for Masques and Plays at Court.* Percy Simpson and C. F. Bell, eds. London: Oxford University Press, 1924.

2240 ANGLO, Sydney. "The Evolution of the Early Tudor Disguising, Pageant and Mask." *RenD,* n.s. 1 (1968), 3–44.

2241 ANGLO, Sydney. *Spectacle, pageantry, and Early Tudor Policy.* Oxford-Warburg Studies. London: Oxford University Press, 1969.

2242 BERGERON, David M. "The Elizabethan Lord Mayor's Show." *SEL,* 10 (1970), 269–85.

2243 BERGERON, David M. "The Emblematic Nature of English Civic Pageantry." *RenD,* n.s. 1 (1968), 167–98.

2244 BERGERON, David M. *English Civic Pageantry 1558–1642.* Columbia: University of South Carolina Press, 1971.

2245 BERGERON, David M. "Medieval Drama and Tudor-Stuart Civic Pageantry." *JMRS,* 2 (1972), 279–93.

2246 BERGERON, David M. "Symbolic Landscape in English Civic Pageantry." *RenQ,* 22 (1969), 32–7.

2247 BERGERON, David M. ed. *Twentieth Century Criticism of English Masques, Pageants and Entertainments: 1558–1642: With a Supplement on Folk-Play and Related Forms by H. B. Caldwell.* San Antonio, Texas: Trinity University Press, 1972.

2248 BERGERON, David M. "Venetian State Papers and English Civic Pageantry, 1558–1642." *RenQ,* 23 (1970), 37–47.

2249 BOYLE, Harry H. "Elizabeth's Entertainment at Elvetham: War Policy in Pageantry." *SP,* 68 (1971), 146–66.

2250 BRENNECKE, Ernest. "The Entertainment of Elvetham, 1591." *Music in English Renaissance Drama.* Pp. 32–56. **See 457.**

2251 CUTTS, John P. "Original Music to Browne's Inner Temple Masque, and Other Jacobean Masque Music." *N&Q,* 199 (1954), 194–5.

2252 DeMOLEN, Richard L. "Richard Mulcaster and Elizabethan Pageantry." *SEL,* 14 (1974), 209–22.

2253 DENT, Edward J. *Foundations of English Opera: A Study of Musical Drama in England During the Seventeenth Century.* Cambridge: Cambridge University Press, 1928.

2254 EWBANK, Inga-Stina. " 'The Eloquence of Masques': A Retrospective View of Masque Criticism." *RenD,* n.s. 1 (1968), 307–28.

2255 FAIRHOLT, Frederick W. *Lord Mayors' Pageants.* London: Percy Society, 1843–44.

2256 GORDON, D. J. "Poet and Architect: The Intellectual Setting of the Quarrel Between Ben Jonson and Inigo Jones." *JWCI,* 12 (1949), 152–78.

2257 HELM, Alex, ed. *Eight Mummers' Plays.* London: Ginn, 1971.

2258 MORSE, J. Mitchall. "The Unity of the Revesby Sword Play." *PQ,* 33 (1954), 81–6.

2259 NICOLL, Allardyce. *Masks, Mimes and Miracles: Studies in the Popular Theatre.* New York: Harcourt, Brace, 1931.

2260 NICOLL, Allardyce. *Stuart Masques and the Renaissance Stage.* London: Harrap, 1937.

2261 ORGEL, Stephen. "*Florimène* and the Ante-Masques." *RenD,* 4 (1971), 135–53.

2262 ORGEL, Stephen. "The Poetics of Spectacle." *NLH,* 2 (1971), 367–89.

2263 ORGEL, Stephen, and Roy STRONG. *Inigo Jones: The Theater of the Stuart Court.* 2 vols. Berkeley: University of California Press, 1973.

2264 RAMSEY, Stanley. *Inigo Jones.* Masters of Architecture Series. London: Benn, 1924.

2265 REYHER, Paul. *Les Masques anglaises.* Paris: Hachette, 1909.

2266 SABOL, Andrew J., ed. *Songs and Dances for the Stuart Masque: An Edition of 63 Items of Music for the English Court Masque from 1604 to 1641.* Providence, R.I.: Brown University Press, 1959.

2267 STEELE, Mary. *Plays and Masques at Court During the Reigns of Elizabeth, James and Charles.* New Haven: Yale University Press, 1926.

2268 SULLIVAN, Mary Agnes. *Court Masques of James I.* Lincoln: University of Nebraska Press, 1913.

2269 TIDDY, R. J. E. *The Mummers' Play.* Oxford: The Clarendon Press, 1923.

2270 WAITH, Eugene. "Spectacles of State." *SEL,* 13 (1973), 317–30.

2271 WEDGWOOD, C. V. "The Last Masque." *Truth and Opinion.* London: Macmillan, 1960. Pp. 139–56.

2272 WELSFORD, Enid. *The Court Masque.* Cambridge: Cambridge University Press, 1927.

2273 WELSFORD, Enid. "Italian Influence on the English Court Masque." *MLR,* 18 (1923), 394–409.

2274 WITHINGTON, Robert. *English Pageantry.* 2 vols. Cambridge: Harvard University Press, 1918–20.

INDEX

INDEX

INDEX

INDEX

INDEX

INDEX

INDEX

INDEX

INDEX

INDEX

INDEX

NOTES